The Complete Selling System

Sales Management
Techniques That Can Help
Anyone Succeed

Upstart Publishing Company, Inc.
Dover, New Hampshire

For Shaun and Doug, who have taught me more than they can imagine and bring me great joy.

Published by Upstart Publishing Company, Inc.
A Division of Dearborn Publishing Group, Inc.
12 Portland Street
Dover, NH 03820
(800) 235-8866 or (603) 749-5071

Library of Congress Catalog Card Number: 92-64010

Printed in the United States of America
10 9 8 7 6 5 4 3 2 1

Book design by Brad Robeson

For a complete catalog of Upstart publications call (800) 235-8866

Preface

There are many books on the subject of selling and management. Bookstores are full of them, and most provide excellent concepts, strategies and techniques. However, there are no books (at least not to my knowledge) dealing with the specific subject of managing sales performance. I find that surprising because it is such an important topic with which so many sales managers need help.

My sales management seminars often include people whose roles range from managing only salespeople to multiple management responsibilities including sales. I begin by asking the participants to tell me the major issues facing them in managing their salespeople. This question is very important because I want to address the issues they face on a daily basis so the seminar will have as much impact as possible on their management performance and provide concepts, tools and techniques they can use the very next day.

The issues they raise about salespeople are the same from seminar to seminar:

> "I can't get them to do what I want them to do."
> "They work hard but just don't make enough sales."
> "I can't seem to get them to make the right number of sales calls."
> "We seem to be making enough calls but sales are not what they should be."
> "It takes new people too long to get started."
> "Forecasts are inaccurate. They keep telling me such and such account will buy in the next few weeks but it doesn't happen."
> "They don't seem to be motivated enough. How can I get them motivated?"
> "I have no idea if they are doing the right things."
> "They don't have a plan and when I try to give them one, they don't follow it consistently."
> "I sell through representatives (or agents). It's almost impossible to get them to do what I need them to do."

"When our store has a lot of people looking at the merchandise, my salespeople have trouble determining which of them are most likely to buy big ticket items. They focus too often on those least likely to buy."

"We sell medical supplies and some of my people have a very hard time getting through to doctors."

"Government agencies are a major market for us but we don't have a GSA contract and find it difficult to compete with companies that do."

"The property and casualty insurance business is very competitive today and my salespeople don't know how to get prospects interested in what my agency can do for them. That's why we have so much turnover."

"We sell strictly by telephone. We give our salespeople a script to follow that we know works, but I'm not sure they use it all or use it consistently."

These comments represent the frustration most managers with sales responsibility face on a daily basis. As a result of working with salespeople and sales managers for the past twenty-seven years and consistently hearing these comments, several things have become obvious to me:

1. There is a right and a wrong way to approach a sale. Most salespeople need to be kept focused on a regular basis to do it the right way. Otherwise, they will approach a sale their own way, which is most often the wrong way.

2. The best sales organizations are those that are best managed. A sales organization with good salespeople who consistently do what is expected by sales management is far more successful than one with "superstars" who operate almost independently. The latter may create sales but they also can create chaos and long-term problems in the organization. These range from "bad orders" that require too much after-sale administration and cause customer relations problems to disharmony within the organization. One of my clients had a salesperson who consistently exceeded sales quotas but refused to complete the reports management needed and was always late to sales meetings. The sales manager felt he was being taken advantage of, in spite of the superstar's sales successes, and the other salespeople wondered why the manager didn't do something about the two problems. They questioned his ability to manage effectively.

3. Effective sales management means developing or providing a selling system that works and then managing that system. It's more important and much easier to make a system work than simply to try to get people to work. Manage the process.

These three principles when set in motion and consistently followed can make pluses out of negative situations that sales managers face. Instead of the frustrating remarks mentioned earlier, managers now are able to say:

"My salespeople do what I want them to do."
"We know now why sales are not what they should be."
"I know exactly how long it takes new salespersons to get started and whether they will make it or not after one month or so on the job."
"Forecasts are pretty accurate. When they tell me such and such account will buy in the next few weeks, it usually happens."
"My people are highly motivated, and I know how to keep them that way. I now know if they are doing the right things in a selling situation."
"They have a plan and follow it consistently."
"I sell through representatives (or agents). They do what I need them to do."
"I can now control my accounts much more effectively, and my sales have increased dramatically."
"My salespeople use the script we provide on every telephone call and it works."

You too can make the same kinds of comments because this book will help you develop a successful system and make it work. Perhaps you are presently doing some of the things described in this book. You may not be doing any of them. By doing them all and doing them consistently, sales performances will improve. You will be in control of your sales organization in ways you never were.

Acknowledgments

Judy deMont who is the kindest person and best retailer in the business. Darrell Reeder who helped me more than anyone can know. Dick Dunbar who constantly focuses on business fundamentals with uncanny objectivity and fairness. Bob Gatti whose encouragement and support has always been a great source of strength. Jim Winters who knew just how to measure the important sales activities. Don Wile, John Peterson and George Carlisle who let me make mistakes and helped me learn how to correct them. Howie Ulfelder, old and trusted friend, who knows as much about successfully managing a business as anyone I know and treats his employees like family. Joe Savino, a great salesperson and philosopher who makes the tough times much easier.

Contents

Chapter 1
Focus on the Fundamentals

The top salesperson for a large insurance company was asked why she was so successful. She replied that the insurance company knew more about selling insurance than she did so she did everything she was told to do. She never skipped any of the details necessary for selling her company's programs—she never stumbled during the course of a sale because she never ignored the basics. She did what "worked" and was successful.

This book provides concepts, strategies and techniques to help you improve the sales performance of your salespeople or your own sales performance by ensuring that you or your salespeople always do all the basics.

It is a myth that successful salespeople are those with the best "personalities", people who are brash and naturally outgoing. The most successful salespeople are those who follow the basic sales routines day in and day out.

This book is written for three kinds of people: First, managers who manage all types of functions in a business such as finance, administration, marketing operations, engineering, personnel as well as sales. Second, sales managers. Third, salespeople who want to "take control" of and eliminate those things that get in the way of top-notch sales performance.

The many books on sales and sales management are written from a variety of points of view, but none focuses on a singularly critical issue: how to improve sales performance by disciplining for consistency in behavior—doing what you should do or getting your salespeople to do what you want them to do, *always*.

Here are some of the day-to-day questions I am asked in my seminars:

> "My salespeople work hard but simply aren't selling
> enough. How can I get them to sell more?"
> "I can't get my salespeople to do what I want them to do."

"We've provided sales training. But I can't tell if it has made any measurable difference."

"We're closing one out of every ten selling situations. Why aren't we closing four, or five? How can I find out?"

"We get a lot of people through my store every day but I don't know what percentage of them buy and what we can do to improve sales."

"Our salespeople's forecasts are not even close. How can we correct that?"

"My salespeople make a lot of sales calls but the orders aren't there. What's wrong? How can I find out?"

"I want to add salespeople (or representatives). How many should I add? How do I find out?"

"One of my salespeople continually performs below quota. Why?"

"I hire only experienced salespeople, but they don't perform the way I expect. Why not, and what can I do about it?"

"When I question whether a salesperson is making enough sales calls (or question any aspect of performance), I always run into some kind of confrontation. What can I do about it?"

"I have provided all kinds of training and sales support materials but this doesn't seem to make much difference."

"It has taken one of my salespeople a full year to become productive. Is that too long? How can I find out?"

"We sell through manufacturer's representatives. How can I get them to improve performance? They are independent business people."

The solutions to these problems are not universally understood. That is the reason for this book. It provides the solutions to these problems and more by focusing on two basic concepts:

First, sales managers really can't manage salespeople—they can only manage their salespeople's performance. Second, managing sales performance means managing the basics.

Many sales managers have complained to me about such intangible problems as the attitude, energy level, work ethic, motivation, dedication, sense of urgency and skill levels of their salespeople, to name but a few. These are problems of manufacturer's representatives, dealers and distributors as well.

The real problem lies in trying to "fix" these intangibles. It's not that simple. Attitudinal problems are due to a variety of causes, mainly psychological or personal. Managers can effect some changes by counseling their people (discussed in detail in Chapter 7), however, as a sales manager you are not a psychologist. You don't have the time or expertise to change salespeople's personal situation and/or psychological make-up. Most attempts in this direction fail, or the change typically lasts only a short period of time, perhaps less than one month. You do, however, have the time and, with the aid of this book, will have the expertise to change salespeople's performance.

You have become aware of these intangible problems because they have in some way negatively affected sales performance. Since that is true, the poor performance is what must be corrected. Correcting salespeople's performance means, quite simply, "getting them to do what you want them to do." Remember, it's easier to change performance than to change people.

Managing Sales Performance Means Managing the "Basics"

The *basics* are all of those things you or your salespeople must do constantly and consistently for successful selling. They are the steps in any selling system that constitute a model for a successful sale.

The reason many salespeople are unsuccessful is that they don't do the basics—the small but essential things—constantly and consistently. They don't trip over the sale itself, they trip over one or more of the many small things that are essential to a successful sale.

The McDonald's chain of fast-food restaurants is a perfect example of doing the basics constantly and consistently. Ray Kroc, the chain's founder, developed one model of a successful fast-food restaurant. He experimented with different methodologies until he had one that worked at peak efficiency. He then franchised it across the United States to a variety of independent business people with the strict stipulation that they were to follow the model exactly. Why? Because it guaranteed success. He got each franchisee to work the model, the system, and has built an incredibly successful business. He knew the right way and the wrong way to do things in that business and avoided the wrong things. Can you imagine the image McDonald's would have if each owner was free to do whatever he or she wanted? It would be chaotic. Customers would never know what to expect from one store to another.

Selling is the same. You will never know what to expect from one sales interaction to another or one selling situation to another without a clearly defined "system" that ensures the right things are done each and every time. All successful enterprises require this consistency. It doesn't matter which of the following types of selling you do:

business to business, to government agencies, to non-profit agencies, to institutions (schools, hospitals or libraries), by direct mail, by telephone, to individuals (insurance, financial services, securities, etc.), retail, to professionals (doctors, attorneys, architects, etc.).

This "system" is necessary for you regardless of your type of management: full time sales manager, wearer of several hats including managing sales manager or are a salesperson yourself.

In all areas, it is by developing and managing a successful model, or system, and ensuring that all sales personnel understand the system and their roles in making the system work that brings success.

Somehow, sales seems to be a mystery to many managers. They don't know how to get their hands around it so that they can develop a system, a model of the successful sale, and make it work over and over again.

In most companies, senior executives are able to provide a solution to a problem in the production, finance, personnel, engineering, marketing and administrative areas. It might not always be the right solution, but one readily surfaces. That is not true for sales. Most senior executives don't know how to solve sales performance problems.

This book shows you, step by step, how to develop a successful sales model or sales system and how to make it work effectively and efficiently on a consistent basis. One that will make it easy for you to identify performance problems in advance and head them off. I provide examples of different types of sales organizations to illustrate how a system is developed and managed. The answers to these core questions that I will raise provide the foundation for a selling system:

1. What do you want your salespeople to do? (just "quota performance" is not enough as you will see)
2. How will you know that they are doing what you want?
3. What will you do if they aren't performing to your expectations?

What Is a Selling System?

A selling system is a combination of a company's sales cycle (from initial customer or prospect contact to a sale or order), its sales managers and its salespeople. One element cannot work effectively and efficiently without the other two.

The sales cycle is often known as the sales process. The sales cycle is comprised of those activities that must be performed by salespeople between identifying potential prospects and closing the sale. They are the critical in-between steps that are absolutely necessary to securing the order or making the sale. The steps will differ for different types of selling, for different products and different services but the need for a step-by-step process is still the same for all businesses.

The sales cycle is like any other process—for example a manufacturing process. In a manufacturing process, each step is of equal importance, leading to a quality finished product. If one of the steps is done incorrectly or left out, the product does not pass the quality check. By the same token, if salespeople are skipping steps in the sales process or doing them sloppily, the results are similar—no closes and lost orders. Such failures are readily recognized by prospect comments such as:

> "We've decided to stay with our present supplier."
> "We are going to hold off until next year. Talk to us again in November."
> "Your price is too high. The competition was much lower."
> "We just don't think the return justifies the investment."
> "It's going to be tough to get budget monies."
> "I really can't make the decision and the higher ups have said 'no.' "
> "Call us in two to three weeks. We'll have a decision then."
> (But they don't, and the sale drags on, and on and on.
> "I want to think about it for a while" (and they're never heard from again.)

It's frustrating to hear these kinds of comments at the end of the sales process when so much time, effort and, often, financial expense have gone into the selling effort. It's especially frustrating when you know that something was missing in the handling of these accounts, but you're not sure what it was. It makes you question whether these accounts could have been handled more effectively or were they not worth the time, effort and expense in the first place.

The Real Issue

It is not that the responses listed on this page aren't legitimate. These prospects had valid reasons for making them. The real issue is that your salespeople should have uncovered them much earlier in the sales process.

It is easy to determine early in the selling situation:

1. If a prospect is willing to do business with you—to change suppliers if necessary

2. When the prospect will be ready to "buy" and what might make the purchase more urgent
3. Whether or not price will be a major issue. If it is, what it will take to justify the purchase
4. How return on investment be measured. Can your products and services meet return on investment criteria?
5. Whether monies are available or not. Can the prospect afford to make the purchase?
6. Whether you are dealing with the person who makes the decision, influences it or has no say in the decision at all
7. Whether the prospect is really ready to act on your recommendations if you fulfill what the person you are dealing with wants and/or needs

It is not only easy to get the answers to these questions—it is a must. If they had been asked and one or more of the responses had been negative, your salespeople would have been in a position to decide:

- to pursue this prospective buyer now because he or she is very likely to buy now or soon
- to put this prospective buyer on the back burner for now and concentrate on working with people who are most likely to buy now.
- to forget this situation altogether.

This is known as "qualifying a prospective buyer." A qualified person or company is not defined simply as one who uses or could use your products and services. That is only a part of the real definition. The definition must also include that they:

- have a need for your products and services, and have told your salespeople when.
- are they willing to do something about it.
- are willing to do it with you.
- have told your salespeople what it will take to get them to do it.
- can afford it.
- have told your salespeople who really makes the decision and who has a major influence on it.

Prospective buyers must be qualified by the fuller definition—they are the ones with whom you want your salespeople to spend the most time. The definition holds for all types of selling mentioned earlier.

Most salespeople spend far too much time with unqualified prospective buyers. It is time consuming and unproductive. This brings us to why it is so important to develop and manage a selling system.

The selling process has been represented as a "funnel" for many years. *Strategic Selling*, a book by Robert B. Miller and Stephen E. Heiman that presents national accounts selling strategies, uses the funnel to illustrate managing time effectively by spending time most wisely. This funnel works much like those you use to put oil in your car or any liquid into a narrow-necked bottle. I am convinced that most sales managers and salespeople don't know how important the funnel representation is. By putting the steps in any sales process into a funnel, it becomes obvious that prospective buyers have to be weeded out as salespeople move through the process.

Figure 1.1 shows a generic sales funnel where there are eight steps in the selling process. Only the most qualified prospective buyers go through the entire selling process. It begins with Step #1—Identifying the highest priority prospective buyers in a market or markets. Many salespeople are required to identify these prospective buyers, which creates a major problem. They can spend far too much time trying to find out if the high priority buyers have been identified rather than spending time *selling* to those who are. This step is a marketing function—not a sales function.

It's much like hiring a new employee. You can put an ad in the local newspaper and receive calls and/or resumes from perhaps hundreds of people. Some will be qualified for the job, but most will not. You have to take the time to sort through them all, which is very time consuming. Or, you can use an employment agency who will screen out unqualified candidates and send you the names of only those who best fit the job description.

A friend of mine is in the venture capital business. He told me that the funnel didn't apply to his business because identifying the best investment potentials from a pool of hundreds of applicants was an art, not a science. His business was different! After we discussed it, he was amazed to find that the funnel did apply to him. He had a set of criteria for weeding out unwanted investments (Step 1 in his funnel) so that hundreds of applicants became fifty potential investments. He had another set of criteria that reduced the fifty to ten (Step #2 in his funnel), and those ten went to Step 3 in his funnel. It became an "art" when it was time to select two or three from those ten. Up to that point, it really was a science. And these applicants were trying to sell him, not the other way around. The funnel concept truly applies to all types of businesses.

Figure 1.1
Generic Sales Funnel

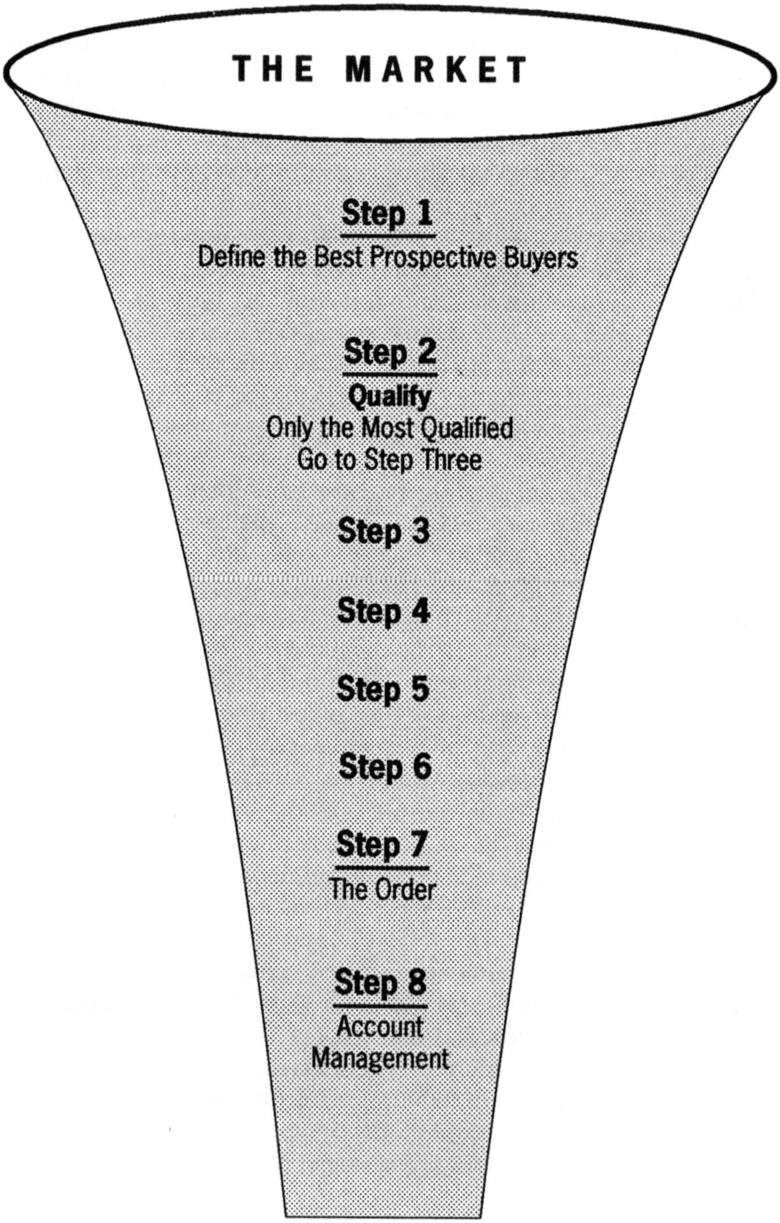

THE MARKET

Step 1
Define the Best Prospective Buyers

Step 2
Qualify
Only the Most Qualified
Go to Step Three

Step 3

Step 4

Step 5

Step 6

Step 7
The Order

Step 8
Account
Management

In Figure 1.1, "the market" at the top of the sales funnel indicate that there are a great many prospective buyers. The lowest priority prospective buyers should be narrowed down before your salespeople meet with them. Advertising is one way to do this. Direct mail is another.

Step 2 is the qualifying step. This is the most critical step in the sales funnel. It is where your salespeople must decide with whom to spend time, whom to put on "hold," and who are not worth their time at all. It is a difficult decision to make for many salespeople because they tend to look at every prospective buyer as a high priority and, with good intentions, proceed through the rest of the selling steps with their fingers crossed, hoping it will work out. However, the objective is to spend time with only the most qualified prospective buyers. The most successful salespeople I have met are dogged qualifiers who refuse to spend time with prospective buyers who haven't told them they will buy if they see or get what they need.

One of my clients told me about a salesperson who once worked for him. This salesperson was selling a computer system that cost $25,000 and was the only salesperson successfully selling this product because he asked all the qualifying questions in the first few minutes of the first sales call and, based on the responses, either proceeded with the sale or left. Period!

Figure 1.1 shows that more screening has taken place and only the most highly qualified prospective buyers continue through the balance of the funnel steps—just as it should be. The funnel continues to narrow from step 3 to step 8 as more prospective buyers are "weeded out" for one reason or another. But the weeding out is not nearly as pronounced as in Steps 1 and 2 because these prospective buyers were well qualified.

How Many Steps Should There Be?

The number of steps depends on the types of selling you do. It may be 1, 3, 5, 8, 12 or more.

One of my clients, Acme Northeast in Boston, sells graphic arts papers, films and chemicals to graphic arts shops throughout the country by telephone. Their salespeople have a four-step sales funnel for getting new business. One business-to-business sales company has twelve. A retail oriental rug client has eight. The steps for each of these as well as many other types of selling environments will be described in detail throughout the book.

The last point to be made about the sales funnel here is that the remaining steps become much easier with a well-qualified prospective buyer. The salesperson will go through the remaining steps because each step is essential to helping the prospective buyer get what he or she wants. In this way the salesperson is continuously moving closer to the order (or the sale).

In other cases, unqualified prospective buyers are most often simply going through the motions. It is activity for activity's sake for the salesperson. Activity is appropriate if it leads to a predictable objective. It is inappropriate if it is done just to say it was done.

Many salespeople try to convince unqualified prospects to see a demonstration or a sales presentation. The objective is not to sell prospective buyers on one or more steps, it is to sell product and service advantages using the steps as the vehicle to get the sale.

A Poor Alternative

The alternative to narrowing prospects to those most likely to buy now is to have a sales funnel that looks like Figure 1.2. Everyone goes through all the steps, regardless of how well qualified they are, because the qualifying step is ignored or done very poorly. Steps 3–6 show that most prospective buyers fall out at the bottom while only a very few orders or sales are secured. It is clearly a terrible waste of time and resources.

If the funnel you used to pour oil into your engine was like Figure 1.2 most of the oil would go on your engine and the pavement below while only a small amount would go into the engine. It would create a mess. A mess is created when your salespeople deal with unqualified prospective buyers.

In both figures, closing the sale is the next-to-last step. Many sales managers have told me that they have salespeople who can't close the sale—get the order. My question to them is "you mean that these salespeople can't ask the customer to make a decision to buy?" The answer in a great majority of cases is, "Oh sure, they ask but the prospective customer says 'no'—they just don't get the business."

The point is that closing the sale is not the problem. Further questioning revealed that the prospective buyers weren't well qualified to begin with. You will see in future chapters how the sales funnel can help you identify accurately where sales performance weaknesses exist so the right actions can be taken to address them. But the first order of business is to be sure you have identified the right performance problem. If the sales managers that I just talked about had spent time and money teaching their salespeople how to close, they would have addressed the wrong issue and the problem would still exist.

Figure 1.2
Sales Funnel When Qualifying Step Is Ignored

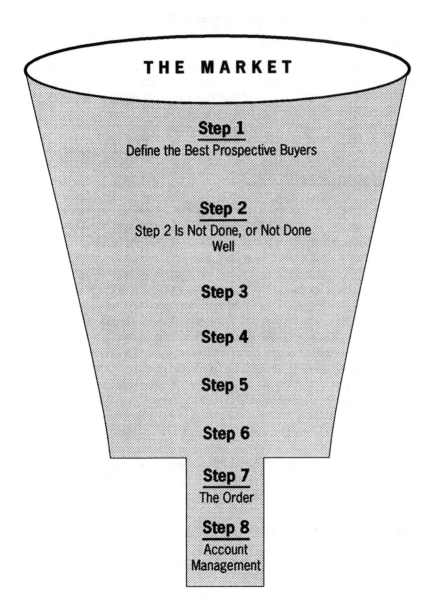

The last step is account management, which many companies use effectively to protect their customer base and generate incremental business in each account.

What Is the Sales Manager's Role in the Funnel Process?

Sales managers must identify the steps that comprise his or her sales process. Performance standards and activity levels must be established, a system to measure their effectiveness and efficiency developed, and the parameters of a "good sales call" defined. The system must be kept simple and straightforward. Chapters 2–4 will show you how to do each of these.

The Salesperson's Role

Salespeople must utilize those selling skills and strategies necessary to move efficiently and effectively through the steps of the sales process. Examples of the right kinds of selling techniques will be used throughout the book as well.

Many sales managers ask me, "Why can't all my salespeople be like my top performers?" It is because between 10 percent and 15 percent of all salespeople will do well regardless of the support they are given. They just "have it." Between 10 and 15 percent won't be successful regardless of the support they are given. They are at the bottom and will ultimately fail. Finally, between 70 and 80 percent of all salespeople need to be kept focused all the time. Left to their own devices, they will not do what they are supposed to do consistently. They want to be successful but either don't know how to be or become lazy in their habits. They need and want help. They are a sales manager's toughest challenge. But the rewards are greatest if their performance can be improved. If you have one salesperson at 150 percent of quota and three at 75 percent, you will achieve greater rewards by getting the latter three to perform at 100 percent than trying to get the top performer to reach 200 percent.

Measuring Results

The system must be monitored by sales managers on a regular basis so that appropriate corrective actions can be taken to ensure that performance stays at standard or above. Many examples will be given later to illustrate the kinds of measurements you will need.

There is a logical process to everything. The objective is to get each of your salespeople doing the right things at every step of your sales funnel and with every account. Obviously you will not "sell" every qualified prospective buyer who goes through your sales funnel. Strange things can happen in a selling situation. Things may change. But you will significantly increase the percentage of prospective buyers who actually *do* buy.

As an example, a baseball player who gets 20 hits for every 100 times at bat hits .200. If he has 200 "at bats," he will get 40 hits—twice as many—but still only bat .200. Since there are only so many times to "come to bat," the player's objective must be to increase his percentage to really improve his performance. It is the same for your salespeople.

Chapter Summary

The sales funnel is the "roadmap" that takes you from the first to the final step of the sale. It is important that your salespeople do the following in every selling situation:

- Accurately define where they are in the sales funnel—it is the only way to know where to go next.
- Describe to you what they must do to go to the next step—what actions need to be taken to keep the sale moving in the right direction.
- Manage and control each step by implementing specific skills and strategies.

If *they* do these things, here's what happens:

- Less time is spent with unqualified prospective buyers and people who can't make the buying decision.
- Fewer repeat prospective buyer contacts are made for the same purpose.
- Greater success will be achieved in competitive situations.
- More progress will be made on each interaction with the prospective buyer.
- The sales cycle (the time from the initial prospective buyer contact to a sale) will become shorter, with fewer "no" or "we'll wait a while" decisions.
- Less discounting will occur.

If *you* manage and control your salespeople's performance at each funnel step, here's what happens:

- You'll know in advance if sales goals will be met (and have time to take corrective action before it's too late).
- You will identify more accurately and objectively performance weaknesses in advance and head them off.
- You can then select the right course of action to correct the weakness.
- You can deal effectively with manufacturer's representatives to achieve sales goals.
- You will improve your salespeople's closing ratios—get a better hit rate.
- You will be assured your salespeople are spending time with the right prospective buyers and doing it effectively and efficiently.

The next six chapters describe the following in detail:

1. How to establish your funnel steps (Chapter 2)
2. How to establish what activities must be performed at each step (Chapters 3 and 4)
3. How to establish activity goals for each step that will predictably lead to a "sale" (Chapter 5)
4. How to monitor activity for improved performance (Chapter 6)
5. How to develop your salespeople for improved performance and what to do (and when) if performance doesn't improve (Chapter 7)

Examples of various types of sales funnels for various selling environments will be used to show how they improve the ability to manage sales *performance* in order to improve sales. They are illustrated throughout the book and are summarized in Chapter 8. Examples of selling techniques and strategies that you and your salespeople can use to improve overall performance at each step of the sales funnel are described as well.

Remember that the primary objective is to ensure that you and your salespeople consistently do the basics—the steps that are essential to a successful sale. Don't stumble because of the pebbles—they are easy to manage.

Chapter 2
Developing the Sales Funnel Steps

This chapter has one objective—to have you develop the steps in your sales funnel so you can better focus your efforts on where you want to go. It provides an easy-to-follow guide to developing them that will ensure that none of your steps is missed. As each step is discussed, detailed examples will be given for two companies with other examples of different kinds of selling environments. A brief description of the two companies follows:

ABC Software. ABC Software has developed and sells a software product and associated services. Their primary markets are sales and marketing oriented companies. This product allows multiple personnel to share (using ABC's own network) critical sales and marketing information that is either unavailable to them now or unavailable on a timely basis. It helps all appropriate personnel manage the selling and marketing effort.

Because of development and ongoing servicing costs, their selling price begins at $30,000. It increases depending on the number of workstations linked to the network. Many "stand-alone" database systems sell for much less although they don't have the features and capabilities of ABC Software's product. Consequently, ABC's product isn't justifiable unless there is the potential for a minimum of thirty workstations. Even then, the per-station selling price will be $1,000, not including the hardware.

There are many steps in ABC's sales funnel.

American Chemical Company. American Chemical has several divisions. One of them manufactures and sells a chemical product, an oil additive, that is used by oil refineries and many smaller companies who work with oil products. The primary benefit of this product is to maintain oil fluid and engine performance at peak efficiency between severely high and low temperature changes.

The buying decision is typically made by a committee, although American Chemical's product must meet established specifications before it is considered for use in oil products.

There are many steps in American Chemical's sales funnel as well, and they are very different from ABC Software's steps.

ABC Software and American Chemical have gone through the process of establishing their sales funnels to manage sales performance better. Managing sales performance means managing the steps that must be accomplished to secure a sales order. If you don't know what your steps are, it is impossible to know what went wrong when one of your salespeople doesn't get the order after working with a prospective buyer for some number of weeks or months.

Imagine planning to drive from Boston to Los Angeles, getting in your car and simply heading west on the turnpike. Imagine how difficult that trip would be, especially if you had never done it before. You wouldn't just "head out" for Los Angeles. What you would do is to decide things such as:

> When you want to get to Los Angeles
> What route(s) you will take
> What cities you will stay in overnight and when you need to reach each city to ensure you are on target for your arrival in Los Angeles. If you are a day late getting to your last city before Los Angeles, you will most likely not reach Los Angeles as planned.
> What you will do if you miss a scheduled city on time
> What you should take along for emergencies (food, water, flashlight, spare radio, etc.)

It would be your roadmap to reaching Los Angeles and reaching it on schedule. The sales funnel is your roadmap to meeting sales targets successfully by following specific steps.

The sales funnel keeps your salespeople focused on those critical steps. They will know what they have to do to be successful. It is a myth that just because salespeople have sales experience, they know what to do in the sales funnel. In fact, they probably don't know there is such a thing as a sales funnel in the first place. "Sales experience" only means that they have held a sales job—it doesn't define how good they were at it. In the great majority of cases, salespeople do not do what they should do consistently. They need a roadmap to follow.

You will have to help them stay focused. Left to their own devices, most salespeople will skip steps or avoid the most difficult one—the qualifying step. The definition of the qualifying step and why it is difficult will be discussed in detail as will the reason why most salespeople spend too much time on the easy steps.

Your sales funnel becomes a formula for success. Each step of the formula must be performed in every selling situation. It is your responsibility to ensure that it is done. When interviewing prospective salespeople, you can explain exactly what they will be expected to do. It eliminates the surprises that can occur when you assume or hope they will do what is supposed to be done, or when they assume something different from what you have in mind. Clearly setting the expectation is a critical piece of the hiring process. You want hard-working salespeople who can and will adapt to your selling environment. Your sales funnel is the heart of that environment.

Establishing Your Sales Funnel

You will develop your steps and list them in this chapter. There are several activities that must be accomplished at each step so you can be certain it was accomplished effectively and efficiently. They will be discussed in detail in Chapter 3 where you will identify those activities for each step in your funnel, but references will be made to them in this chapter. It's difficult to discuss the definition of a step without referring to the types of activities typically found in that step. ABC Software and American Chemical will be used to illustrate certain activities.

These activities generally fall into the following types:

- An act to be performed (a product demonstration or sales presentation, for example)
- Statements to be made to a prospective buyer (opening statements on the initial call, various benefits statements, etc.)
- Questions to ask a prospective buyer (to determine his or her degree of interest in your product or service, for example)

Figure 2.1 is a funnel worksheet. You will use this worksheet to fill in the steps in your funnel. Refer to it as you go through the rest of the chapter.

The most important activities will be performed in Step 2— Qualifying. Although the qualifying step can be accomplished in a relatively short period of time (10–60 minutes in one, or at the most, two sales interactions), it requires the greatest emphasis by you and your salespeople because it determines which prospective buyers go

Figure 2.1
Funnel Worksheet

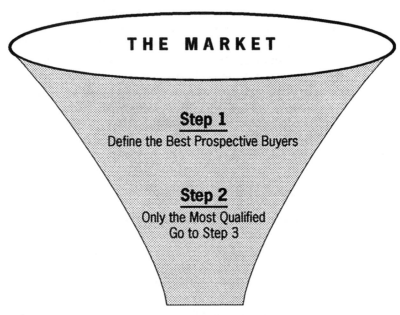

THE MARKET

Step 1
Define the Best Prospective Buyers

Step 2
Only the Most Qualified
Go to Step 3

Your Step 3 _____

Your Step 4 _____

Your Step 5 _____

Your Step 6 _____

Your Step 7 _____

Your Step 8 _____

Your Step 9 _____

Your Step 10 _____

Your Step 11 _____

Your Step 12 _____

Your Step 13 _____

Your Step 14 _____

Your Step 15 _____

Other _____

_____

_____

_____

_____

to Step 3 now and which do not. And that is the critical decision your salespeople must make.

Most salespeople don't want to make that decision, however. They prefer to go through the steps regardless of whether the prospective buyer is qualified or not, hoping the sale will happen. This is the reason why managers are surprised when accounts don't close when forecasted (or they aren't surprised because it happens so often)— why they find critical information about the prospective buyer missing and why they discover that there was an abundance of activity with no real purpose except to generate activity.

The qualifying step must get at all critical information. This is the hard part of the funnel for most salespeople because it requires them to address business and personal issues with a prospective buyer when they are most comfortable discussing product or service specifics. They typically want to jump to Step 3 or allow the prospective buyer to take them right to Step 3.

A majority of time is spent in the sales funnel steps that follow the qualifying step. As you will see, their function is primarily to address issues determined in the qualifying step. The number of steps varies from industry to industry, market to market and product/service to product/service. There are no fixed number of steps.

Steps 1 and 2 are filled in on your funnel worksheet. That is because they are almost always the same for all businesses. You will begin filling in your funnel steps at Step 3.

Step 1

The first step is to decide on which kinds of prospective buyers you want your salespeople to concentrate their efforts. Your business plan has defined your primary markets and market segments. Now you must decide specifically what kinds of businesses or people in those markets (or market segments) are most likely to buy your product or service. What kinds of companies or people should you target? Here are the types of questions ABC Software considered in making that decision:

1. Do they have a minimum of thirty salespeople?
2. Are all salespeople located in one or two offices where information can be shared easily and in a timely manner or are they spread throughout the United States where sharing information is most likely a problem?
3. Do they have regional offices where information can be distributed to the salespeople in that office from one

workstation or will each salesperson need to be provided with a workstation?

4. Does our data base indicate what companies have typically bought from us based on these types of parameters: annual sales volumes, numbers of salespeople, multiple sales offices across the United States, increasing vs. flat or decreasing sales volumes.

This kind of analysis will help your salespeople focus on the types of accounts that are most likely to buy your product or service.

This is all that will be said about prospecting and targeting accounts because it is a marketing function, not a sales function. Many companies rely on salespeople to find the prospects who are most likely to buy. This is a mistake because it takes them away from their primary function—qualifying prospective buyers and performing the steps necessary to secure an order or make a sale.

The more time salespeople spend searching out prospective buyers, the less time they have to sell. This is not a major problem in retail sales because salespeople typically have little control over who comes through the door. However, many retail organizations require their salespeople to make follow-up phone calls to prospective buyers who did come into the store at least once. This will be discussed in more detail in Chapter 3.

Figure 2.2 shows the effect of screening an unlimited number of people or companies who could or do use your products and services.

Step 2—Qualifying

This step also applies to all selling companies or individuals who sell regardless of products or services provided and the markets and market segments to which they are selling. The qualifying step typically consists of asking informational, knock-off and business oriented commitment questions to determine whether to pursue this prospective buyer now, put the prospective buyer in a futures category or forget the situation altogether.

Informational Questions

These are issues about things such as the prospective buyer's size, annual revenues, credit rating and so on. ABC Software's Informational Questions are those listed on page 19. Other selling environment lists will be presented in Chapter 3. For some selling businesses, the answers to these questions may be important in the decision to go ahead or forget this account before a face-to-face sales interaction occurs. American Chemical and ABC Software both want

Figure 2.2
Step 1: Defining the Best Prospective Buyers

their salespeople to pre-qualify prospective buyers on the telephone first.

Knock-Off Questions

ABC Software needs to know if this prospective buyer can "technologically" use their product or service? For example, is there sufficient memory in their computer to load, store and run the software product without a costly hardware upgrade? This is known as a "knock-off" issue because the prospective buyer couldn't make ABC Software's product work technologically unless the question was answered affirmatively.

Business-Oriented Commitment Questions

Does this prospective buyer need what your company offers? Will it measurably improve its business in some way? If it won't, or they don't perceive that it will, it's difficult to create a selling situation. It's most often a question of whether or not they have "pain." If you have a bad headache, you would probably take aspirin. If it persisted, you would see a doctor. But you wouldn't take any action if there were no pain.

Is this prospective buyer willing to do something about the pain? Will the buyer consider you as a supplier and when does the buyer want the pain to go away?

What do you have to do to make the sale—what must be done, shown, and/or proven? What must be done, shown, and/or proven will take several of the steps in the stem of the funnel (that is, from Step 3 down).

Do you know who the decision maker and the decision influencers are? The former can say yes even if the latter say no, or no even if the latter say yes. However, decision makers usually respect the opinions of decision influencers who can't make the "yes" decision but can kill it. This applies to large companies where many buying influences are involved as well as small retail stores and real estate firms, to name but a few.

One of my clients, Newton Oriental Rug Fair, sells oriental rugs, for the most part, to couples. One is the decision maker and one is the decision influencer. It is important for their salespeople to determine which is which so they can focus on the decision maker while addressing the decision influencers likes, wants and concerns as well. It is the same for real estate salespeople.

What are the business concerns of the decision maker and influencers—the concerns your company, product and/or service address?

For ABC Company, the vice president of sales and marketing (the decision maker) may be concerned about "unnecessary costs associated with not sharing pricing information with their salespeople on a timely basis that causes complaints, credits and angry customers (who might go elsewhere), while the sales manager (a decision influencer) may be concerned about whether the salespeople will deal with the impact of automation and make it work as a part of their daily routine.

For American Chemical, the decision committee may be concerned about whether the product will perform consistently from batch to batch (chemical products are produced in batch lots) while the production manager may be concerned about the impact of changing products on his production schedule. These concerns are also very different. They aren't at cross purposes, and both concerns must be addressed.

For Newton Oriental Rug Fair, who have two stores, the decision person may be primarily concerned about the cost of the rug while the decision influencer may be concerned only about color.

For real estate firms, the decision maker may be concerned about how the kitchen is laid out and how much cabinet space there is while the decision influencer is concerned with the size of the yard because the lawn has to be mowed, leaves raked and walks and driveways shoveled or plowed. It is essential to gather all of this information so the concerns can be addressed during the course of the selling process.

What are the buying criteria? On what basis would they make the buying decision if it had to be made today? Some examples are: price, quality, service, vendor's reputation, after-sale support, user references.

What is the decision process? If the prospective buyer wanted to "buy" today, what administrative and sign-off levels must he or she go through to issue a purchase order or arrange financing? It could take up to another 30–60 days after verbal approval depending on the type of business. Before your salespeople can get the answers to these questions, they must interact with the prospective buyer by phone, face-to-face, or both.

The Initial Call

For our purposes, the "initial call" is defined as a sales interaction with a prospective buyer who has not bought a product or service from you. Several sales interactions may have been made with no success. In a few cases, a prospective buyer will call your company and that is an initial call situation as well. There are two critical points to bear in mind on the initial call (the first is why the second is so important):

1. An invisible wall exists between a salesperson and the prospective buyer on the initial sales interaction. The prospective buyer is wary: a decision to deal with a salesperson (probably the umpty-umpth salesperson that day) is at hand. This makes the prospective buyer immediately uncomfortable because people typically don't like to make decisions. It's the kind of discomfort most people feel when they walk into a retail store and the clerk asks, "Can I help you?" The immediate reaction is something like "No thanks, just looking" and a desire to leave the store. The best way for prospective buyers to deal with that discomfort is to get the salesperson off the phone or walk out of the store.
2. It is essential, then, to make an opening statement during the initial sales interaction that stresses the value of your product or service. Specifics about them are to be avoided at this point.

Most buying decisions are made on the basis of real or perceived value. If a business or personal problem is solved or a need is satisfied it's a good business or personal decision to do it—it has value. If it doesn't solve a business or personal problem or satisfy a business or personal need, it's a bad business or personal decision to do it—it has no value.

ABC Software's salespeople open an initial sales interaction with a discussion about the impact of their product on a prospective buyer's information flow, not with product specifics.

American Chemical's salespeople open the initial sales interaction with a discussion about the impact of their product on oil performance during cold and hot weather, not with product specifics.

Newton Oriental Rug Fair's salespeople open the sales interaction by asking, "Is there a specific size I can direct you to?" from a distance, and let the prospective buyers start looking for the size they want right away in an unthreatening way. They don't walk right over to the prospective buyer(s) and ask, "Can I help you?"

Product or service specifics are appropriate further down in the sales funnel as you will see. They can only create the following kinds of problems at the qualifying step:

- The prospective buyers probably won't see any difference between what you offer and what they are doing now because they don't see any value—so they ask what your price is.
- When price becomes the focal point this early in the sales funnel, it's almost impossible to ever get back to the value your product provides that justifies the price. It's too late.
- Prospective buyers defend their comparable product or service because they may have chosen it. In any event they often feel some ownership for and bias toward it. This situation can become argumentative.

As an example:

Prospective buyer: "What is your pricing?"
American Chemical salesperson: "What are you paying now?"
Prospect : "You tell me first. I want to see if you're in the ballpark."
ACs: "$150 a barrel."
Prospect : "Is that for a 50-gallon drum?"
ACs: "No, it only comes in 10-gallon drums."

Prospect: "Well, we only buy 50 gallon drums—it's more economical and shipping costs are less."
ACs: "You wouldn't consider going to 10 gallon drums?"
Prospect: "No, we're paying substantially less than your price on a 50-gallon drum basis."
ACs: "We might be able to do something on the price."

This so-called "selling situation" is going nowhere. It's not even a selling situation—it's a negotiating situation. It's hardly appropriate to begin "negotiations" five minutes into an initial sales interaction. The salesperson is negotiating with a prospective buyer who may not be interested in the product in the first place. This type of situation happens much too often.

Examples of the right kinds of statements are presented in Chapter 3 where the details of specific activities are discussed.

The Telephone Contact

In the case of telephone sales, all questions must be asked on the phone. Outside salespeople selling in non-retail selling environments should phone the prospective buyer or the initial sales interaction buyer for two reasons—and two reasons only: *First,* to qualify them based on your informational and knock-off questions. *Second,* to make an appointment (assuming this prospective buyer satisfies the informational and knock-off criteria).

They shouldn't sell your product or service or let the prospective buyer draw them into a conversation about your product or service or price. That gives the prospective buyer reasons not to make the appointment—the only way to relieve his discomfort. Some examples describing how to deal with these situations are provided. They may be much different from the way your salespeople handle them now. If you want them to try using these examples, expect some resistance because the procedure is new and, therefore, uncomfortable. Practice is necessary—spend some time practicing them with your salespeople.

One method of avoiding product or service discussions at this point is to say: "My presentation is a visual one. It will only take a few minutes of your time to present it and ensure it addresses the issues most important to you. When would it be convenient for me to see you?"

One method for avoiding the price issue is to say: "It's difficult to say just what the price would be because it can vary depending on just what your particular needs are. And if our product or service doesn't do what you need it to do, it really doesn't matter what it costs, wouldn't you agree?" Now your salesperson can say (again):

"As I said, my presentation is a visual one. It will only take a few minutes of your time to present it and ensure it addresses the issues most important to you. When would it be convenient for me to see you?"

Once the appointment is confirmed, your salesperson is now ready to make the face-to-face call. On this call (which is discussed in detail in Chapter 3), the business-oriented questions must be asked. The answers to these determine whether to go to Step 3 now or designate this prospective buyer as a low-priority account.

Classification Systems

A word about "account prioritizing" is warranted—defining the most-likely-to-buy prospective buyers. You may have a classification system in place now. If not, you might consider the following example of a classification system:

Priority A—An account where all decision makers and influencers have agreed to the decision, the paperwork has been completed and in process. Waiting for a Purchase Order to be generated in the next five to ten days. They should be called on at least weekly.

Priority B—We have met the decision makers and influencers, they have met all qualifying criteria, and have completed Steps 3 and 4. Steps 5–7 will be completed within 30 days. They should be called on at least weekly. *Note:* This account should move to Priority A in 30 days.

Priority C—We have not met the decision maker and influencers but have talked to the decision maker by phone. This account meets the informational criteria, and the decision maker wants to meet with us. Call frequency to be determined when it becomes either a Priority B or D. *Note:* You and your salesperson should determine if this account should be moved to Priority B or D after the initial contact.

Priority D—They do not have need for our product or service for 6–9 months. We should follow up with a phone call in 120–150 days.

Classification System Advantages

A classification system provides a tracking method to ensure accounts are moving in the proper direction. It also keeps the "pipeline" or the sales funnel full at the top. If there are an insufficient number of Priority Bs and Cs in the funnel, quota might be achieved this month but the next two to three months potential becomes suspect.

You should ask your salespeople for monthly forecasts. Based on this classification example, only Priority A accounts should be on it since they are the accounts your salespeople expect to close in 30 days. If any other Priority accounts are on it, they should be immediately challenged.

You should expect a weekly itinerary and call report to be submitted to you. The itinerary tells you which accounts will be called on during the upcoming week. You want to know if the Priority As are there (weekly calls required). If there are an insufficient number of Priority Cs in the funnel, you would expect to see prospecting activity. You might also want to know whether Priority B calls are planned.

The Call Report tells you what actually happened during the past week. You can determine if what they said they would do was really done. It's important to know what your salespeople did this past week. But it's most important to know what will happen next. It's your method for ensuring they are planning the right types of calls on the right types of accounts. An Itinerary and Call Report Sample is provided in Chapter 6. It should be obvious by now that Steps 1 and 2 require a great amount of emphasis and skill.

Step 3

You will notice that in Figure 2.2 the steps following Step 3 are not filled in. That is because the balance of the steps will depend upon some decisions you will make based on the discussions about each of them. One of four things should occur at Step 3:

1. Survey—when it is necessary to gather information for a presentation and/or demonstration
2. Product or service presentation—if a survey is not necessary, you will go directly to a selling presentation
3. Product or service demonstration—it either follows a presentation or can replace it if the prospective buyer wants to go directly to the demonstration step.
4. Trial or Product Test—typically American Chemical's step 3— they need to have the product approved while several other steps are taking place. The product trial or test is American Chemical's demonstration.

It is Newton Oriental Rug Fair's demonstration as well. They let a prospective buyer take a rug home for a day or so to see how it looks and feels in the room where it will go. This greatly enhances their chances for a sale.

The Survey

A survey quantifies the business benefits your product or service provides for use in the presentation and/or written proposal. It determines the impact of your product/service on the prospective buyer's organization in dollars and cents.

ABC company enables customer users to share information on a timely basis. One example of this type of information is "pricing changes." If their salespeople don't have these pricing changes when they are put in place, their customers might pay too much, and credits must be issued once the error has been caught. This is an unnecessarily expensive and time-consuming activity. ABC's product eliminates it.

If ABC knows how often this happens and what the dollar impact to the prospective buyer is, they can quantify the impact of acquiring their software package on this one issue alone. Clearly there would be several other measurable issues ABC will impact as well. The survey determines what those issues are and what the business impact of ABC's product is in dollars and cents.

A survey identifies the concerns of decision influencers. Presentations must address the concerns of the decision maker and decision influencers. The survey identifies other pertinent details, and determines what needs to be done to implement the program and what kind of time it will take.

For ABC, some examples are:

- Identifying the type of host computer in use so start-up programming development time and needed resources can be planned
- Identifying the types of reports managers and users will want.
- Determining when the prospective buyer can actually implement ABC's solution. The buyer may want to do it next month, but three months will be needed to put the program in place in all locations.
- Determining the number of user locations (both in regional sales offices and the home office for sales and marketing)
- Determining whether all users will have terminals and what information will be disseminated manually? How will that impact the timeliness of shared information?

If a survey is necessary in your sales environment, write it in step 3 of the Funnel Worksheet.

Presentations

A presentation is needed when one or more people in the prospective buyer organization want to hear about your product or service simultaneously, or when your product or service cannot physically be demonstrated. For example, if you are selling advertising, samples of previous work can be seen and references are important to the selling effort. There is nothing to demonstrate that proves you will provide the kinds of services your client wants.

If a presentation is a necessary piece of your sales environment, write it in as Step 3 if you didn't enter the survey or Step 4 if you did.

People like proof that what they are getting will do what was promised. A demonstration is used to prove that your product or service will do what you say it will do. It can be demonstrated that the product actually does it. ABC Software can demonstrate that their product will provide the results a prospective buyer wants. The prospective buyer can see it for himself on a computer terminal screen. American Chemical and Newton Oriental Rug Fair can only prove what their products will do by a product test or trial. A real estate salesperson has no way to prove that a home is termite free. The prospective buyer will have to hire an expert to know that.

If Step 3 is a survey, Step 4 a presentation and a demonstration, and a product test or product trial is required, write it in as Step 5.

You can see that Steps 3, 4 and 5 depend upon which of the four types of activities are necessary to sell your product or service: a survey, a product or service presentation, a product or service demonstration, or a trial or product test.

The Next Step

The next step might be a proposal that formally states all of the reasons why the prospective buyer should buy your product or service. A proposal is necessary when it will be read by people who will influence the decision and you either can or cannot meet them. It is designed to sell your products and services in your absence. The most dangerous situations exist when a proposal is not a selling document but simply a price quotation and some technical backup data.

The problem is that when someone asks your contact(s) why the company or individual should invest in your product or service, no real business or personal reasons are available for your contact(s) to fall back on. The proposal should be a selling document, otherwise, it may hurt your selling effort. If a proposal is important in your selling environment, make it your next step and write it in along with the appropriate step number. The elements of a selling proposal are detailed in Chapter 3.

Follow-up

Some follow-up is clearly required and is probably the next step. Follow-up is essential in all selling situations. The qualifying step determines whether the balance of the steps are worth your salespeople's time and effort.

The follow-up step is where all of the hard work put in so far can go awry. There are several reasons why:

1. The prospective buyer's interest can begin to wane as time goes on. The positive effects of the presentation and/or demonstration wear off.
2. A competitor can come in and steal the sale. Have you ever had a prospective buyer tell you, "We're going to think about it" after a demonstration or proposal and later learn the prospective buyer bought a competitive product or service? It happens all too often.
3. In American Chemical's case, the product could fail in testing. If they don't know about it, or haven't provided to be notified in such case, this sale is lost, and it's too late to do anything about it. Prospective Newton Oriental Rug buyers might have someone say to them, "I know where you can get a better deal" while they have the rug on trial. If their salespeople don't follow up, their sales could be lost as well.
4. If the demonstration was poorly done, the prospective buyer could visualize it as being a hindrance rather than a solution to a problem. If ABC tries to demonstrate how simple the system is to operate and then makes it look complicated by many code-intensive keystrokes, the prospective buyer will think "my people will never be able to make this work."
5. People in the prospective buyer organization can change positions, or new people can come in. If that happens, it may mean going back to the qualifying step. But your salespeople had better know about it. Or a Newton Oriental Rug prospective buyer could come for a second look at a rug and bring someone else along who may have a different set of concerns and interests.

Follow-up is critical. A specific schedule for follow-up should be established (you will do this in Chapter 3). Here's how ABC Software approaches it: Identify who has primary interest in seeing the program work and communicate with this person as follows:

- Hot or tight time frame project—short lead time— once a week then daily within a week of expected decision
- Long lead time project—six to nine months away—once every month at least
- Manage the process—don't assume it's on track— know where the proposal is always
- If problems occur, what can we do to help make it work?

In all probability, you should write follow-up in as the next step in your funnel. Write it in along with the appropriate step number.

Acceptance/Rejection

The next step will most likely result in proposal acceptance or rejection. It will result from your salesperson attempting a close. This then becomes the closing step and needs little explanation (sample closing techniques are presented in Chapter 4). Everyone knows that the close is designed to get a buying decision.

If your proposal is accepted, the funnel is complete except for the last step. If it is rejected, here are some reasons why that sometimes happens (it doesn't mean the sale is lost, just on hold).

1. The prospective buyer has one or more objections to going ahead with your proposal. These must be gotten out of the way.
2. The prospective buyer wants a better price, or better terms and the like—it's the negotiating piece of any selling environment.
3. There is a legitimate budgetary problem.

Your salespeople should be able to handle the first two depending on the degree to which they are allowed to negotiate. The budgetary issue may require some rethinking about sale terms or alternative payment plans (leasing, for example) on your part.

The close is most likely your next step. Write it in along with the appropriate step number.

The Last Step

Account management is the final and essential step. It is much more than simply account maintenance—stopping in to see how things are going. It requires managing the account. There are several things that must happen in the account management step:

1. When communicating with a customer, look for new business opportunities.
2. Ensure proper start-up. This is where some real hand holding is needed. Help your customer during this transition. He'll be your friend forever.
3. Monitor product application. Ensure that your product or service is providing the value your customer expects. If the customer is not getting full benefit, you open the door to competition.
4. Look for opportunities to recommend new or different products.
5. Maintain an on-going relationship at all levels.

Maintaining a customer relationship is more than dropping by. Talk to the decision makers (the higher ups) on all calls. It's important to reconfirm the value they're getting from your products and services. Get your contacts to spread the word about your product's success. Remember, they can also spread the word about its lack of success as well. Make sure they are committed to your company and are happy with the results they're getting from your product and your service. There is always threat of competitive encroachment. Look for it. Gain leads for other new selling opportunities and references to support your benefit statements with new accounts and market/product intelligence.

Account management is most likely your next step. Write it in along with the appropriate step number.

There may be some steps that you will add because they are specific to your business. However, the funnel should include the ones described in this chapter. Your funnel steps—your roadmap to the sale—are complete. Chapter 3 deals with how you will determine if each step was performed well by your salespeople. It is the beginning of the evaluation process—determining where performance is deficient and deciding what to do about it.

Figure 2.3 shows the Acme Northeast sales funnel. As you recall from Chapter 1, they sell by telephone only. Their products are graphic arts papers, films and chemicals that are used in various pieces of equipment in small commercial print shops, camera departments, large commercial typesetters, magazines, newspapers and chain shops like PIP (Postal Instant Press) to name one.

Acme Northeast's sales funnel is very different. They advertise infrequently because it doesn't produce a sufficient return on their investment. Their salespeople telephone all commercial print shops, government printing agencies, newspapers and companies who have their own in-house graphics departments. Telephoning is Acme Northeast's Step 1. They qualify each account on that initial sales interaction by using the following script, which has proven to be very successful

Figure 2.3
The Acme Northeast Sales Funnel

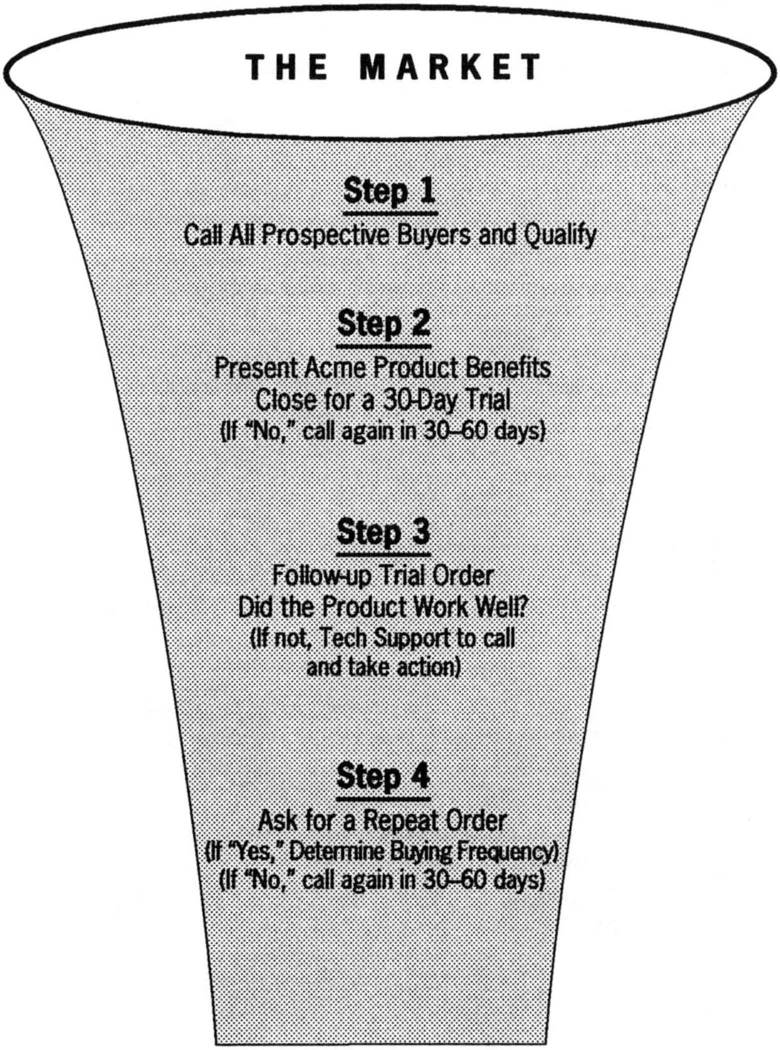

THE MARKET

Step 1
Call All Prospective Buyers and Qualify

Step 2
Present Acme Product Benefits
Close for a 30-Day Trial
(If "No," call again in 30–60 days)

Step 3
Follow-up Trial Order
Did the Product Work Well?
(If not, Tech Support to call
and take action)

Step 4
Ask for a Repeat Order
(If "Yes," Determine Buying Frequency)
(If "No," call again in 30–60 days)

Salesperson: "May I speak to the person responsible for your typesetting or camera department?"
Prospective Buyer: "That's me."
Salesperson: "This is (Name) from Acme Northeast. Are you familiar with Acme Northeast?"
Prospective Buyer: "No, I'm not."
Salesperson: "We are the largest telemarketing graphic arts dealer in the United States, specializing in all pre-press supplies. I'd like to ask you a question—if we could offer you an equal or superior (name product) at a very competitive price, perhaps even less than you're paying now, is there any reason why you wouldn't do business with us?"
Prospective Buyer: "No, I'd consider it."
Salesperson: "What would you suggest we do to get you started using our materials—what's the next step?"

The prospective buyer now will tell the Acme salesperson what it will take to get their business—that's what happens. The first question ("If we could . . . , would you . . . ?") is the most important qualifying question. It immediately determines if there is an opportunity to do business. After the salesperson gets to this point in the script, he or she has to interact with the prospective buyer based on the buyer's responses. But this question is critical and will be used in a variety of situations throughout the book. It determines whether time will be spent with this prospective buyer now or to say "thank you very much" and go on to the next call. Your salespeople should make it a part of their sales interaction early in the sales process. It is critical.

If the account is qualified, they then go to Step 2, where they present the benefits of Acme Northeast as a company and the products that apply to each account. They then close for a "30-day free trial." If the answer is "no," they enter the name of the account in a calendar planner for follow-up in 60 to 90 days. Acme Northeast knows that it may take three to four calls before a prospective buyer agrees to try their product. They will send a short proposal only if the prospective buyer requests it. It is not a formal part of their process at this point although they are considering it.

Steps 1 and 2 are accomplished on the initial sales call. They then go to Step 3—follow-up on the trial order. They want to be sure the prospective buyer has tried it and that it worked as expected. If there are any problems, they refer the account to a technical support group who calls to resolve any problems. It sometimes requires replacing a product but the technical support people can resolve the problem in 75 to 80% of the cases.

Step 4 is to ask for a repeat order. If they get one, they ask the customer (who is now no longer a prospective buyer) how frequently he or she will be ordering. They enter that on a customer account card and put the next order date on the appropriate date in their calendar planners. If the prospective buyer says "no" to a repeat order, they ask why and try to get the order again. If unsuccessful, they will plan to call again in 60 to 90 days. Steps 3 and 4 are accomplished on the same telephone call.

Chapter Summary

Managing sales performance means managing the steps that must be accomplished to secure a sales order successfully. Since you now know what your steps are, you are on your way to knowing what went wrong when one of your salespeople doesn't get the order after working with a prospective buyer for some number of days, weeks or months.

The sales funnel is your roadmap to meeting sales targets successfully by following specific steps. The sales funnel keeps your salespeople focused on those critical steps. They will know what they have to do to be successful. It is a myth that just because salespeople have "sales experience," they know what to do in the sales funnel. In fact, they probably don't know there is such a thing as a sales funnel in the first place.

"Sales experience" only means that the salespeople have held sales jobs—it doesn't define how good they were at it. In the great majority of cases, salespeople do not do what they should do consistently. They need a roadmap to follow.

You will have to help them stay focused. Left to their own devices, most salespeople will skip steps or avoid the most difficult one—the qualifying step. You now know why the qualifying step is so important and yet misused if used at all most of the time.

You have begun building a formula for success. You can ensure that each step of the formula is performed in every selling situation. When interviewing prospective salespeople, you can explain exactly what they will be expected to do. It eliminates the surprises that can occur when you assume or hope they will do what is supposed to be done, or when they assume something different from what you have in mind. Clearly setting the expectation is a critical piece of the hiring process. You want hard-working salespeople who can and will adapt to your selling environment. Your sales funnel is the heart of that environment. Make the funnel work for you as it has for so many companies.

Chapter 3
Establishing Your
Sales Funnel Activities

T he sales objective itself is not as important as the process to be followed in reaching the objective. The roadmap to the sale is the process by which you or your salespeople are most likely to get the sale. A critical part of the process are those activities that must be performed at each step of the sales funnel. Establishing the activities in your sales funnel is detailed in both chapters 3 and 4. Since the qualifying part of the funnel is the most critical step, Chapter 3 will focus on qualifying. Chapter 4 will cover the balance of the funnel steps.

These two chapters have one objective—to have you develop the activities that must be performed at each step of the sales funnel you developed in Chapter 2. As you will see, these activities become the performance standards for each step and, consequently, the means of determining if each step was performed to standard.

Ensuring any standard is met is a management responsibility. The activity standards you are about to develop will give you the tools and measurements by which to manage sales performance. However, you have to do it on a regular basis. More will be said about this in Chapter 6.

These standards help you identify one of the most critical issues in managing sales performance—where does a sale typically go wrong. If you can objectively (rather than subjectively) identify where your salespeople have gone wrong, several important sales management benefits result.

First, you can anticipate potential problems and head them off. For example, American Chemical Company's salespeople are required to follow up on a hot or tight time frame project weekly and then daily within a week of the expected decision. If that isn't done, it's possible that the decision won't be made as agreed; or that some new factors may enter the picture, such as a decision influencer who would like to review the competition once again. If the salesperson doesn't know about it because follow-up wasn't done according to the standard, the sale could be in trouble.

If the salesperson did know about it, however, the issue might have been averted. There is no guarantee that it would have, but there's a chance. There's no chance if the salesperson didn't know about it.

One Acme Northeast telephone salesperson had a closing ratio of 1 order for every 25 telephone calls at the end of one month when the company average is 1 for every 12 telephone sales calls. This salesperson isn't using the script at all, is using it ineffectively or isn't closing with sufficient persistence.

Since you will know what the standard is, you can ensure your salesperson meets it by monitoring the activity.

Second, you can identify specific training requirements. For example, certain information must be gained at the qualifying step. If that information isn't gathered on a regular basis by one or more salespeople, further skills training is needed. Training will be discussed in detail in Chapter 6.

Third and finally, you can eliminate activity for activity's sake. If the required information is not gathered at the qualifying step, the sale will most likely continue through the rest of the process based on inaccurate or incomplete information and you will be surprised when the order doesn't close.

One example of incomplete information might be the identification of the decision influencers. If they aren't all contacted, one might kill the sale. You want to know that early in the process—not after weeks or months of effort, time and expense. Or a real estate salesperson might not find out what a couple is really looking for in a home (perhaps the couple is not sure or doesn't agree) and shows them several homes over a one to three-week period with no positive results, hoping upon hope that they might see something they like. That might happen but it is a risky investment of the real estate salesperson's time.

Eliminate this kind of problem by ensuring all of the information to be gathered is actually gathered. If it isn't, send your salesperson back to get it. It's important not to go from one step to another until you are certain that all activities have been performed to standard.

That summarizes the major *benefits* of defining the activities for each of your sales steps. The sales funnel concept offers more advantages that will be discussed in subsequent chapters.

You will now begin defining the activities that must be performed at each of your steps. It was stated in Chapter 2 that these activities fall into three types:

1. An act to be performed (a product demonstration presentation, for example)
2. Statements to be made to a prospect (opening statements on the initial call, various benefit statements, etc.)
3. Questions to ask a prospect (at the appropriate times throughout the sales process).

You will develop these for each step in your sales funnel from the examples presented on the following pages. Step 1, as you will recall from Chapter 1, is a marketing function, not a sales function. It won't be discussed here.

Step 2—Qualifying

In Chapter 2, you began filling in your steps at Step 3. However, the qualifying step (Step 2) is the most critical step. It is important that you define your qualifying activities. (See Figures 3.1 and 3.2)

Sales management and salespeople too often believe that a prospect is qualified simply because their product and/or service is used. For example, American Chemical Company at one time assumed that simply because Exxon used oil additives, they were qualified to buy from American Chemical. Nothing could be further from the truth. All American Chemical knew was that Exxon used oil

Figure 3.1
The American Chemical Sales Funnel—Step 1

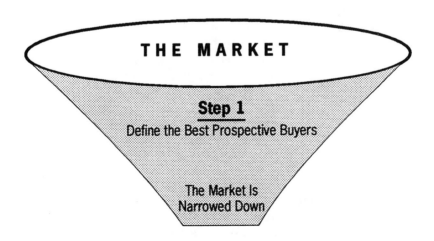

THE MARKET

Step 1
Define the Best Prospective Buyers

The Market Is
Narrowed Down

additives. There was clearly no indication that: Exxon would buy American Chemical's product; American Chemical could supply Exxon's needed quantities (based on American Chemical's manufacturing capacity); or they could approach the current vendor's price (and remain profitable). In fact, Exxon didn't even know who American Chemical was! It is important to determine at the qualifying step whether your prospect will buy from you and if you want to do business with them.

American Chemical's funnel step activities, along with other selling environment examples, will be shown to assist you in developing your activities: Each of their steps will be listed and discussed; sample sales scenarios will be given to show how the activities should be performed if appropriate; and you will develop your activities for your similar steps.

Figure 3.2
The American Chemical Sales Funnel—Step 2

The activities American Chemical requires in the qualifying step (Step 2) are listed under three categories: prior to the initial sales calls, the initial sales contact, the follow-up sales interaction. Each of these activities will be discussed with emphasis on why they are so important and what information is needed, what questions must be asked, what statements must be made. If that activity is appropriate for your selling process (it most likely will be), write down either the information you want your salespeople to get through questions you want them to ask or statements you want them to make on a separate page. You might want to add other activities if they are not listed here and they are appropriate to your selling process. However, the most common ones are listed under American Chemical's activities.

American Chemical's Pre-Qualifying and Qualifying Activities

1. Prior to the initial sales calls
    a) gather appropriate account research information.
2. In the initial contact on the telephone
    a) Make a value-oriented opening statement and
    b) pre-qualify to determine if a face-to-face meeting is necessary. The call objective is to pre-qualify and, if appropriate, make the appointment only—don't sell on the phone at this point.
    c) Work with "calls in" from prospects and customers based on sales potential.
3. In the follow-up face-to-face sales interaction:
    a) Make a value-oriented opening statement
    b) Confirm those value issues by gaining prospect agreement through the effective use of questions to gain and maintain control of the selling situation
    c) Qualify (included reconfirming pre-qualification information)
    d) Establish the buying criteria—the basis for a buying decision
    e) Gain appropriate commitments
    f) Establish a written agenda
    g) Identify a "Coach"
    h) Identify the next step and its objective

A detailed discussion of each activity follows:

Prior to the Initial Sales Calls

Salespeople should gather appropriate account research information. Some research must be done prior to making a sales call (either on the phone or face-to-face). It makes the call more professional and saves time. For example, credibility is established if your salespeople know in advance what their product line is, how successful their business is and who the key contacts are. American Chemical gathers information from Annual Reports, Industry Journals, American Chemical personnel, company records of previous activity if available, and salespeople from noncompetitive companies who have contacts with this account. Contact with other salespeople calling on your accounts should be one of your strategies—they can provide all kinds of intelligence as well as put your salespeople in touch with key decision people.

The information American Chemical attempts to gather is:

1. What is the prospect's company size—revenues?
2. What kinds of products do they make, what are their primary markets?
3. Who are the key contacts in research, purchasing, production and marketing since one or more of them will typically be involved in the decision process?
4. How many calls were previously made to this account and what were the results?
5. Who is the competition?

If your salespeople should gather information prior to the initial sales interaction, list the information you want gathered. Ten lines are available although you may use fewer or need more:

1. _____
2. _____
3. _____
4. _____
5. _____
6. _____
7. _____
8. _____
9. _____
10. _____

The Initial Contact

American Chemical uses the phone whenever possible, but if a salesperson has only two appointments in a certain location, he or she might make "cold calls" on smaller oil additive users in that area to find out who the decision people are, ask the informational and knock-off questions, and try to arrange an appointment.

Make a value-oriented opening statement. How should salespeople introduce themselves—what should they say on this call to earn the right to ask pre-qualifying questions? They can't just say something like: "I'm with American Chemical Company. We make oil additive products. Would you mind if I asked you some questions?" They must earn the right to ask those questions.

The Intrepid Insurance Agency is a small company with one salesperson (in addition to the owner) who sells Property and Casualty insurance to businesses whose premiums will not exceed $150,000. annually. This salesperson can't call a prospective buyer and say, "My name is Jim Jack, with The Intrepid Insurance Agency. Would it be possible for us to get together and review your coverage to see if it's what you really need?" The answer would, in 98 percent of the cases, be "No!" Salespeople must be more creative to generate interest. But they can't do it if no one shows them how. This applies to both initial phone and face-to-face sales interactions. The opening statement made on the phone should be made during the face-to-face sales interaction as well. The issues are still the same.

Most business and/or personal buying decisions are made because a prospect sees value in going ahead with the decision. Value is described as either the personal or business impact your product or service has on prospects. If it's a good business or personal decision to go ahead with your program because it has value, your customers will most likely do it—they won't if it does not. As stated in Chapter 2, if the prospect doesn't see any value, the decision is typically not made at all. If the prospect doesn't see the value you offer versus your competition, the decision will most likely be made based on price. It is imperative that your opening statement stress the value of your product or service.

American Chemical's salespeople open an initial sales call with a discussion of the impact of their product on a prospect's production flow and consumer satisfaction, not a discussion about an oil additive from a technical point of view.

The dialogue goes something like this:

> Salesperson: "Good morning, my name is ____ , I represent American Chemical Company. We have developed and manufacture products that might improve your oil products production process and guarantee that your customers will receive a product which performs better in extreme cold and warm weather conditions as they have for (name two or three customers the contact would know). Would you be interested in hearing about it?"

A business issues-oriented statement gains attention because it addresses prospect concerns. American Chemical knows from experience that a typical contact is concerned about production rejection rates and satisfied consumers. Consequently, their opening statement addresses those concerns in a general way. Any opening statement should address the typical concerns of the contact and include two or three customers who have enjoyed the value to be derived (it lends instant credibility to the opening statement).

Different people in a prospect organization (research, production, marketing and purchasing) have very different concerns. For American Chemical, these concerns typically are:

1. Research—Will the product perform to specifications and does it have some properties that make it superior in some way to the current product(s) used?
2. Production—Can this product be integrated into the production process quickly and easily and will it perform consistently from batch to batch (so rejection rates will be minimal)?
3. Marketing (and sales)—Does this product have some advantages we can stress to our customers and will they receive a better final product ?
4. Purchasing—Will the product be delivered on time to specification and are the terms and pricing competitive?

The only real technical discussions will take place with research. The balance of the concerns are related to either business or personal issues. Each department wants to improve the business situation (in most cases) and have a personal stake in the outcome of a major decision affecting the performance of the finished product. American Chemical's opening statement addresses them. It is a fairly general opening statement. When talking to each of the decision influencers in different departments, however, statements must be made to address their concerns.

The Intrepid Insurance Agency salesperson was given a script to use on initial sales contacts (by phone). Many salespeople, especially the more experienced ones, generally balk at using a script. They think they know how to sell. The owner of Intrepid Insurance believed that, too, until he saw his salesperson was not getting the desired results.

Using a script is a very powerful way to get a selling situation started properly. Scripts are used by many companies. It's impossible, however, to script an entire sale because the sale won't unfold the way it has been scripted. The moment the prospective buyer asks a question the script doesn't cover, the salesperson is lost and will look like a phony who doesn't know what he or she is doing. But you can script the opening statement when it is designed to determine whether this prospective buyer warrants more of your salesperson's time or not.

If you hire a new salesperson who has sales experience, he or she will not know how to introduce your product or service unless he or she came from a company with similar products and services. Even when that is the case, he or she may not know how to introduce your products and services properly on the initial contact. You should find out through role-play activity (practice selling situations).

We developed the following opening script for Intrepid Insurance that significantly increased the number of appointments made:

> Salesperson: "My name is Jim Jack with the Intrepid Insurance Agency. You probably get lots of phone calls from insurance agencies who promise better coverage and lower premiums. But I can't make that statement because I don't know anything about the kinds of risks you face and what your needs are. However, we offer some interesting packages that have helped many companies like yours (names two or three the prospective buyer would know). The purpose of my call is to find out if we could do the same for you, would you be interested in hearing about them?"

This script was developed to address several prospective buyer concerns. Prospective buyers get inundated with phone calls and mailings from all types of selling companies. Every telephone sales call makes the prospective buyer put up an invisible wall. You probably have done the same thing when a telemarketer calls you at home, or at your place of business. It raises a danger signal: "Oh oh, how do I get rid of this one?" without even knowing if it might be something of real interest to you.

Consequently, the statement "You probably get lots of phone calls from insurance agencies who promise better coverage and lower premiums. But I can't make that statement because I don't know anything about the kinds of risks you face and what your needs are" is designed to break down that invisible wall—and it works.

We then added the statement about helping other companies like the prospective buyer's and named two or three. It's important because prospective buyers like to know who is using the product or service, especially companies of their size and companies they know or with whom they are familiar. If your customers don't want competitors to know they are buying from you, you will have to ask permission before using their names. And it lends credibility to your product or service—it is real and real companies are using it.

We finished with a commitment question, "If we could do that for you, is there any reason why you wouldn't be interested in hearing about them?" It's very important to get that commitment from the prospective buyer early in the sales process.

From this point on, the salesperson must react to the prospective buyer's comments and questions. That can't be scripted.

Figure 3.3 shows the Intrepid Insurance Agency sales funnel.

Figure 3.3
The Intrepid Insurance Agency Sales Funnel

THE MARKET

Step 1
Advertise to Define the Best Prospective Buyers

Step 2
Qualify
Only the Most Qualified
Go to Step Three

Step 3
Sales
Presentation

Step 4
Survey
Prospective
Buyers

Step 5
Proposal
Preparation
and Presentation

Step 6
Issue a "Binder"

Step 7
Review Policy
Deliver Policy

Step 8
Account
Management

Write an opening value-oriented statement for your company and/or products that addresses the typical business and/or personal concerns your prospects have and finishes with a commitment question within the "If we could...is there any reason why you wouldn't?" statement.

_____

_____

_____

_____

_____

_____

_____

The Technical Sell Problem. Many salespeople want to talk about their products and/or services from a technical point of view. Prospects, however, assume that the product will work—otherwise the company wouldn't be in business. As stated earlier, third-party references (satisfied customers) lend credibility to the fact that the product works. The real question is this: Does it have value to this prospective buyer? If it does, go on—if it doesn't, it's time for your salespeople to move on and find prospects for whom it does have value.

Here's what can happen if a prospect engages a salesperson in a "technically oriented" discussion. Incorrect and then correct responses are given for the salesperson:

Salesperson: "Good morning, my name is _____ , I represent American Chemical company. We have developed and manufacture products that can improve the production flow of your oil products and guarantee that your customers will receive products from you that perform better in extreme cold and warm weather conditions as they have for (name two or three customers the contact would know). If we could do those things for you, would you be interested in hearing about them?"
Prospect: (Not answering the commitment question and taking control) "What kind of a product is it?"
Salesperson: (Incorrect) "It's an oil additive product."
Prospect: "I'm very busy right now. Why don't you send me a brochure and I'll look it over."

This prospect has hardly been given a valid reason for listening to the salesperson who, incidentally, believes this response is a pretty good sign when, in reality, the prospect is simply trying to get rid of him/her.

> Salesperson: (Incorrect) "Good, I'll put it in the mail to you today. Can I call you in a week or so to see what you think of our program?"
> Salesperson: (Correct) "It's difficult to describe all of the things our company can offer your company in a brochure. It would be much more advantageous to you if we could get together and let me present just what American Chemical might be able to offer your company, like we have for (name two or three companies he/she would know). Would it be convenient for us to do that later this week?"

Your salespeople should avoid being put off by a prospect. Asking for a brochure is most often a way to get rid of the salesperson because, as was stated in Chapter 2, prospects prefer avoiding decisions, and the safest way to avoid a decision is not to be in a position where one must be made. This is called a stall. Most brochures wind up in the wastebasket or, perhaps, a file drawer where they are rarely looked at again. Two other examples of stalls and suggested responses are:

> Prospect: "We're happy with our present suppliers."
> Salesperson: "I'm sure you are. If you weren't, you perhaps would have called us. Would you give me a few minutes to tell you how we were able to help companies like (name two or three companies he would know)?"
> Prospect: "I don't have time to talk to you now."
> Salesperson: "I'm sure you're very busy. I'd like to ask one question—if we could help you the way we've helped companies like (name two or three companies he would know), would you give me some time later to tell you about it?"

Again, the salesperson is asking for the commitment. It is essential to keep asking the commitment question until it is answered.

The "If we could...is there any reason why you wouldn't?" problem. Getting the "If we could...is there any reason why you wouldn't" question answered is essential. In the last scenario, the salesperson asked the question but the prospective buyer responded with "What kind of a product is it?" The salesperson should have responded as follows: "As I said, it's an oil additive product that might offer your company some interesting benefits as it has for so many of our customers and I'm calling to see if it could offer you the same kinds of advantages, is there any reason why you wouldn't do business with us?"

The initial sales interaction should not end without your salespeople having the answer to that question. The American Chemical salesperson is now ready to pre-qualify.

Pre-qualify to determine if a face-to-face meeting is necessary. The call objective is to pre-qualify and, if appropriate, make the appointment only—not to sell.

Pre-qualifying is a part of the qualifying process but doesn't require that all qualifying information be gathered. It is used to determine if it makes sense to make a follow-up sales call. It is essential to screen out unqualified prospects early in the process. This concept has been and will continue to be stressed in this chapter. It is critical and can't be emphasized too strongly. It is used also to avoid cold calling someone who won't see you without an appointment. It would clearly be a major problem at a company the size of Exxon.

The pre-qualifying questions are typically informational in nature and conclude with a commitment question. The questions are not worded as all salespeople would ask them but indicate the information that must be gathered. They can also be scripted. The initial call is typically made to an identified key contact in production and/or research. American Chemical needs the following pre-qualifying information:

- "Who is your current supplier of oil additives?"
- "Do you have a second source?" Most oil clients second source the products they buy in the event the primary source can't meet a delivery, or a series of deliveries, or have quality problems develop.
- "In what size containers are oil additives shipped to you now?"
- "How do you decide whether to consider another supplier for second sourcing?" This will point the salesperson in the right direction. In most cases, research must approve a product before it will be considered for future use so the salesperson will be directed there if not already speaking with research.
- "What is your decision process? If you were to decide to use or second source an oil additive, what approvals must be gotten and by whom? Who gives the 'OK' once your recommendation has been made?"

The last question is critical in any account where a number of people throughout a variety of departments are involved in the decision. They must all be contacted at the qualifying step. In accounts where one person makes the decision, much less initial effort is required. Buying decisions may be made by a committee or an individual. This is the place to begin finding out. As you will see, it also helps to track an order at the bottom of the funnel.

Many salespeople ask this type of question: "Are you the one who makes the decision to acquire (any product, any service)? The answer is usually "Yes," even though that person may be a decision influencer only. Typically, people like to think of themselves as decision makers whether they are or are not. The problem is that when a contact says "Yes" to the "Are you the decision maker," it can lead the salesperson to focus on that one contact only and miss other critical influencers and the final decision maker. It is a common mistake, costs companies business, and happens all too often.

There always is a final decision maker. For example, purchasing will tell American Chemical that they make the buying decision. However, research must approve the product. Production must be convinced that the product can be easily integrated into the production process and perform to specifications that include acceptable rejection rates. A recommendation is made to a higher management level—vice president of production and/or marketing typically or a committee where these two people have the major clout. They ask such questions as:

"Why do you want to change to American Chemical?"
"Are we sure they can deliver product to spec and on time?"
"What advantages does making this change offer us?"
"What is their track record with other companies?"
"Do you see any potential risks?"
"How does their pricing compare with the current supplier?" If it's more expensive, "why" and "how is it justified?" If it's less expensive, "you're certain we aren't giving anything up?"

This doesn't apply to smaller companies where the decision maker is easy to identify. For example, one of my clients, TravCorps, Inc., in Malden, Massachusetts, is a very successful company in the Traveling nurse business. Many hospitals don't need a full complement of nurses on a full-time basis but do from time to time. Or they may have difficulty getting nurses with various specialties. My client has a listing of thousands of nurses who don't want full-time work but like to travel to different locations and work for from one to three-month stints. The objective is to match the nurses up with assignments they will like at hospital locations they will like.

This company advertises for nurses regularly—they are always looking to add to their list of nurses who will travel. Their salespeople receive calls from nurses inquiring about the kinds of assignments available, pay, housing, benefits, travel reimbursement and the like. Clearly the nurse is the decision maker. They immediately qualify the nurses as follows (there is no pre-qualifying step):

Informational Questions

- "When will you be available to travel?"
- "Have you traveled before?"
- "Where would you like to go on an assignment?" (preferred location)
- "Do you prefer a specific hospital?"
- "Would you consider any other locations?"
- "Do you prefer 8 or 12 hour shifts?"
- "Would you consider the non-preferred shift?"
- "Would you drive or fly to a location?"
- "What are your salary requirements?"
- "Are there any conditions under which a lower salary would be acceptable?"
- "Would you be willing to take a three month assignment or would you prefer one month only?"

Knock-Off Questions

- "Will you be traveling alone?" (Many like to take their families and pets, which creates travel costs and housing problems.)
- "What is your specialty?" (Some specialties are not needed at TravCorp's client hospitals.)

They will also get a sense of the nurse's general attitude toward travel which can be a "knock off."

The Business Oriented Commitment Questions

The commitment question puts the ball squarely in the nurse's court—a decision has to be made. They ask, "If we could offer an assignment in your first location choice today, is there any reason why you wouldn't accept it?" They may not have an assignment in that location today but the nurse must complete an application and go through a reference check before being added to the list and probably wouldn't be ready to travel for a month or two at the earliest. So there is time to find an assignment. The point is they know if this nurse would take the assignment or not. If the answer is "No," they ask, "What would it take to have you accept one of our assignments?"

After getting the answers to these three sets of questions, they will present the advantages of working with TravCorps and answer any questions the nurse might have.

In American Chemical's case, if production, purchasing and research can answer the initial call questions satisfactorily, the buying decision will most often be made then. Purchasing, then, really doesn't make the decision. They simply influence it. That is why the question, "What is your decision process?" is worded as it is. It gets to the heart of the decision process and away from "Are you the decision maker?"

American Chemical's question: "Are you happy with your present supplier(s). Is there anything you would like them to do that they don't do now?" has a special objective. The objective is to find out how the prospect feels about the present supplier. In most cases the response will be that "they are happy." However, asking, "Is there anything you would like to see them do differently?" (or words to that effect) can raise some concerns that might give you a foot in the door. For example, the response might be, "We wish they would test their batches more accurately." This is an opening to probe for the impact of not testing every batch on the prospect's business—such as, "We have to do it to ensure we don't have production-run failures. It takes up a lot of time on our part. We wish we didn't have to do it, quite frankly."

This gives their salespeople the opportunity to probe further and ask a question such as "If we could show you how our testing procedures eliminate the need for our customers to do it, is there any reason why you wouldn't be interested in seeing how and also find out what other things American Chemical can offer your company?" This last question is another commitment question—an essential part of every sales process as you must have come to realize by now.

Before discussing commitment questions in detail, list the pre-qualifying information you want your salespeople to gather if pre-qualification is important in your sales process:

1. _____
2. _____
3. _____
4. _____
5. _____
6. _____
7. _____
8. _____
9. _____
10. _____

The business-oriented commitment question is the final question in the pre-qualifying process. It is used to determine, "If we could do something, is there any reason why you wouldn't do something?" and asks the prospect to make a nonthreatening decision. It is a very simple yet powerful selling technique. It can and should be used throughout the sales process as well as in the pre-qualifying step. Most salespeople don't like to ask commitment questions because the prospect might say "No," a very disconcerting response. They feel they have a "live one" and don't want to let go. But commitment questions are critical. You must take the prospect's temperature—find out if he/she is hot, warm or cold. The ideal response is "Yes." Typically, it is "No," or "I'm not sure," but they are desirable as well. If a prospective buyer has no interest in your product or service, you want to know it—and you want to know it as early in the sales funnel as is possible.

In the qualifying process, it is equally important to probe for the reasons behind the answers to your qualifying questions. That is where selling really begins—with a "No," or "I'm not sure." For example, if the response to the commitment question, "If we could eliminate the need for our customers to do it, would you be interested in seeing how and also find out what other things American Chemical can offer your company?" is, "I don't think so. We're pretty happy with our present vendors." That's a "No" and your salespeople should ask a question. The prospect's response will dictate the next question to ask or statement to make. It's obviously impossible to list all possible sales scenarios but one example follows:

> Prospect: "I don't think so. We're pretty happy with our present vendors."
> Salesperson: "May I ask you this? Even if we eliminated the need for you to test every batch, you wouldn't consider us as a potential supplier, is that right?"

Prospect: "I don't think so." (This is an "I'm not sure" response.)

Salesperson: "May I ask you why?"

Prospect: "Well, they have done a pretty good job for us in other areas."

Salesperson: "May I ask you what those are?"

Prospect: "Well, they deliver on time and to spec, even though we do the testing. And if there are any problems, they come in and help resolve them."

Salesperson: "If we could eliminate the testing issue, provide the same level of support and deliver the product on time and to spec, wouldn't you at least consider us?" (Another commitment question)

Prospect: "Well, perhaps we should."

Salesperson: "Why don't we set a time for me to come in and discuss what we can do for your company? I'll be in your area next week. Is Tuesday convenient for you at, let's say, 10:00 AM?"

Prospect: "Yes, that will be fine."

Note: The prospect might have asked about pricing, packaging, or some technical issues. If salespeople respond by talking about one or more of them at this point, the sale could easily get sidetracked. If the discussion is about price, the prospect might say, "That's much more than we're paying now." Then, the salesperson is in trouble. He/she must now try to defend the pricing without having had the chance to discuss what value the prospect will get for that price.

Salespeople should simply say something like, "I'll be happy to go into all of that when we get together. I'm sure you'd agree that the price doesn't really matter if we can't do all of the things you need from a vendor, isn't that true?" They should now ask for the appointment once again. The objective is to get the appointment, not to sell your company or product on the pre-qualifying contact.

One thing might have become clear as you read through the scenario. The salesperson controlled the process by asking questions. It's essential to maintain control by asking questions in two areas so that:

First, the sale moves in the direction your salesperson wants it to go, not in the direction the prospect wants it to go. Prospects can take a sale so far away from the objective that it's all but impossible for the salesperson to get it back on track. Whoever asks the questions is in control. There is no greater frustration in sales than feeling control slipping away because the prospect is dictating the direction of the sale by asking questions and putting the salesperson on the defensive.

Second, salespeople can find an opening—a selling opportunity. It is inappropriate to simply use a script. It is appropriate to address issues the prospect raises. In the scenario, the prospect raised the issue of "having to test incoming products." The salesperson used this opening to make a selling point by asking a commitment question.

The objective in selling is to have the prospect talk. The only way to do that is by asking questions. The entire sales process can be controlled by: asking questions (as was done in the scenario), answering questions with questions, and following every statement with a trial close (an opinion question).

> Prospect: "What does your product cost?"
> Salesperson: "May I ask how much you're paying now?"

> or

> Prospect: "Where do you manufacture your product?"
> Salesperson: "Will that make a difference in your decision?"

Acme Northeast's prospective buyers (from all across the country) ask where they are located. If the salesperson simply replies, "We're located in Boston" and lets it go at that, the prospective buyer might think that it will take many days to get the product delivered and that is unacceptable in the graphic arts marketplace. Since that question is asked almost every time, the salesperson has been "scripted" to respond as follows:

> Salesperson: "We're located in Boston. Does that concern you?"
> Prospective Buyer: "Yes, it will take too long for your products to get to Nebraska."
> Salesperson: "When you order a product, how fast do you need to have it delivered, typically?"
> Prospective Buyer: "In two days."
> Salesperson: "Let me ask you this, if we could guarantee two-day delivery, is there any reason why you wouldn't do business with us today?"

It is critical that salespeople employ these techniques throughout every sale—from beginning to end: ask questions, answer questions with questions, and follow up every statement with a trial close. If your salespeople have difficulty asking good questions, they must be taught how to do it (discussed in Chapter 6).

American Chemical's commitment question is: "If American Chemical could show you a product that would improve performance statistics and give you the quality you expect consistently from batch to batch, would you test it and use our product if it does what we say it will do."

This question assumes the answers to the pre-qualifying questions 1–5 indicate there is sales potential. If they don't, it doesn't need to be asked. It can be asked, but if the prospective buyer doesn't meet American Chemical's pre-qualifying criteria, the response is immaterial (or it should be). Some salespeople will pursue the prospective buyer anyway. That is the major reason why there is so much activity for activity's sake in selling today. It takes a tough-minded salesperson to pre-qualify a prospective buyer out and a tough-minded manager to ensure it is consistently done. But it is essential if you are to concentrate limited time and resources on prospective buyers who are most likely to buy.

Rewrite your pre-qualifying commitment question in the space provided if you have seen something that makes you want to change it, using any of the examples given.

_____

_____

_____

Pre-Qualifying Summary

Pre-qualifying a prospective buyer will save time and money. It can be done on the phone, which saves time because so many calls can made in a short period of time, and telephoning is less expensive than a face-to-face call. Estimates of face-to-face sales-calls costs vary, but it is in excess of $100. per call. That is why the telephone is such an important tool. Some of your salespeople might say they don't like using the phone—they aren't comfortable. When salespeople say they aren't comfortable performing some task, it is usually because they haven't done it before and don't know how to do it. Some training sessions and practice (both in training and on-the-job) will soon eliminate the fear.

If salespeople (or any other employees, for that matter) aren't doing what they are supposed to do, it is for one or more of the following reasons:

1. They don't know what they are supposed to do (addressed in this chapter).
2. They don't know how to do it (addressed in Chapter 6).
3. They aren't directed to do it (the manager's job).

4. They simply can't make it work.
5. They don't care (a tough problem that will be addressed in Chapter 6).

Each of these is a management problem and is correctable. The best salespeople are the ones who diligently qualify because they refuse to waste their time on poor prospective buyers. Since most salespeople aren't the best qualifiers, this step must be managed.

"Calls In"

American Chemical receives calls from a variety of accounts expressing interest in their products on a daily basis. Many request samples. At one point, they were sending out roughly 200 samples per month at an average cost of $15.00 per sample and never knew the results of that activity. There was no follow-up and they didn't know why the samples were requested or what they were to be used for.

This is another example of activity for activity's sake. It is important to pre-qualify these "calls in" to determine whether it is worthwhile sending the sample or not and establish a time for a follow-up call to see what the next selling step should be. American Chemical's salespeople and internal personnel receiving these calls in ask three questions prior to the five pre-qualifying questions presented:

1. "How did you hear about us—what made you call American Chemical?"
2. "What kind of application are you interested in testing our product for? How do you plan to use it?"
3. "Is there a timetable for using this product in your products?"

They then ask the balance of the pre-qualifying questions.

If you receive calls from prospective buyers for literature, sample, pricing, etc., pre-qualify them before doing any of those things.

The pre-qualifying portion of Step 2 is complete. Assuming the prospective buyer meets your pre-qualifying criteria, the next activity is the follow-up sales call. Typically, this will be a face-to-face call. In the telephone sales environment, the entire qualifying process would have occurred on the initial contact call.

The Follow-Up Sales Interaction

The activities in this step are the same, or should be the same, for all selling environments.

Make a Value-Oriented Opening Statement

Refer to Figure 3.4 throughout this chapter.

The opening statement will be the same as that used on the initial contact. This takes place at the qualifying step. It simply should be preceded (after your salespeople have introduced themselves and gotten the usual amenities out of the way) by, "As you may recall, when we spoke last week, I mentioned that..." and then continue with the opening statement, "We have developed and manufacture products that can improve the production flow of your oil products

Figure 3.4
The Follow-Up Sales Interaction

A) Make a value-oriented opening statement
B) Reconfirm the value issues
C) Qualify
   1. Does this prospective buyer need our solution?
   2. Does this prospective buyer want to do something about it?
   3. What do we have to do to make this sale?
D) Establish the buying criteria
   Reconfirm informational questions
E) Gain appropriate commitments
F) Establish a written agenda
G) Identify a coach
H) Identify the next step and its objective(s)

and guarantee that your customers will receive a product from you that performs better in extreme cold and warm-weather conditions as they have for (name two or three customers the contact would know). The reason for this meeting is to discuss how we can do that for you."

Reconfirm Value Issues

Confirm those value issues by gaining prospective buyer agreement through the effective use of questions to gain and maintain control.

> Salesperson: "Would it be important to you to see if we could make your production process more efficient and give you a product that would perform better in extreme cold and warm-weather conditions?"
> Prospective buyer: "Yes." (Confirmation has been established.)
> Salesperson: "Before I go into these issues in detail, would it be OK if I asked you a few questions so I can focus my presentation on your interests and concerns?"

This last question is extremely important. Studies show that a majority of buyers feel salespeople are only interested in selling the product regardless of the buyers' interests and concerns. Buyers want to deal with a salesperson who takes a genuine interest in his/her concerns and interests. It establishes credibility and eliminates the "here's another salesperson who only wants to cram a product down my throat" feeling.

Qualify

Qualify by reconfirming pre-qualifying information—your salespeople should come to these meetings prepared with the questions and answers. Continue with other business-oriented qualifying questions, starting with, "Does this prospective buyer need your solution?" In American Chemical's scenario, the answer is "Yes." The prospective buyer said that "testing incoming products was time consuming" and wished the company didn't have to do it.

In every sales situation, one objective is to determine if there is: pain, latent pain or no pain. There is an identified problem, the prospective buyer has stated it and wants to do something about it. With latent pain there is an identified problem, the prospective buyer may or may not have stated it (in many cases the prospective buyer may not be aware of the problem until enough probing questions have been asked to uncover it). This was American Chemical's situation—the salesperson got the prospective buyer to raise the issue by asking questions. He/she may not have stated, however, that he or she wants to do something about it. If there is no pain, everything is fine and there is no reason to consider a change regardless of what the American Chemical salesperson said or did.

This call, therefore, would not have been made if "no pain" were discovered during the pre-qualifying process. The American Chemical salesperson identified latent pain.

The second business-oriented question is, "Does this prospective buyer want to do something about it?" Obviously, the way to determine this is to ask a commitment question, "If we could help you in the areas I mentioned, is there any reason why you wouldn't do business with American Chemical?"

I have heard hundreds of salespeople say "If we could, would you consider doing business with us" or "If we could, would you be interested?" The problem with these is they don't ask if the prospective buyer would "buy." Almost everyone would "consider it" or "be interested." The objective is not to get a commitment to "consider it" or "be interested." It is to determine if the prospective buyer "has any reason for not doing business" with you. One Acme Northeast salesperson adds the word "today"—"Is there any reason why you wouldn't do business with us today?"

The reason so many salespeople ask if the prospective buyer would "consider doing business" or "would be interested," so they say, is that they are afraid to ask someone to "buy" so early in the sales funnel. But asking someone, "Is there any reason why you wouldn't do business with us" is not the same as asking someone to "buy." It is much softer but achieves a great deal. You will know what the reasons for not doing business with you are so they can be addressed and a decision made whether to pursue this account or not. There can only be one of three answers—"Yes," "No," or "I'm not sure". As was stated earlier in this chapter, these are openings for the salesperson to ask additional questions to find selling opportunities. The answer to this question is not as important as probing the reasons behind the answer, then probing the reason behind that answer, and so on until a selling opportunity becomes clear.

The third business-oriented question is, "What do we have to do to make the sale?" To make the sale, American Chemical typically must

- submit a product for testing.
- follow-up on the testing.
- conduct a survey to determine the impact of their product on the prospective buyer's business.
- make a formal presentation to all decision people (geared to concerns and the basis for the buying decision).

- gain permission for a trial production run.
- follow-up.
- submit a written proposal.
- follow-up.
- close the sale.
- provide account management.

There are two choices at this point: Simply proceed through the funnel by suggesting it to the prospective buyer step by step, or ask the prospective buyer what steps should be taken. This is far more desirable. If the prospective buyer suggests to the salesperson what should happen, he/she becomes committed to the steps. In the typical American Chemical sale, the prospective buyer will ask for a product to test, a presentation, a production test and a proposal. A survey might not be requested but if American Chemical feels it to be sufficiently important, the salesperson will ask, "Would it be helpful if we did a survey so that you can see the financial benefits of using our product?" The prospective buyer becomes committed to each step and will help to make each step effective.

Buying Criteria

The basis for a buying decision, the buying criteria, are those issues the prospective buyer will consider when making a buying decision. If they are not established with each of the decision people, it's impossible to know how to gear your selling benefits. This activity begins by determining their concerns. The typical concerns of American Chemical's key decision people are given here, along with sample scenarios for research and production.

Research—will the product perform to specifications and does it have some properties that make it superior to the product(s) currently being used?

> Salesperson: "We know that our product must meet or exceed your specifications. Is there anything else that you expect from a vendor?"
> Research prospective buyer: "No, I don't think so."
> Salesperson: "If our product does meet or exceed them, would you recommend us to production, purchasing and marketing?"

Production—can this product be integrated into the production process quickly and easily and will it perform consistently from batch to batch so rejection rates will be minimal?

Salesperson: "Most of our clients were initially concerned about how easy it would be to integrate our product into their production system and would it perform consistently from batch to batch. Do you have the same concerns?"

Production prospective buyer: "Yes, we do."

Salesperson: "Do you have any other concerns about doing business with American Chemical?"

Production prospective buyer: "Yes. Where is your product made?"

Salesperson: "Will that be an important factor in your decision?"

Production prospective buyer: "Well, if it has to be shipped across the country, I have some concerns about your ability to get it to us when we need it, especially in emergency situations."

Salesperson: "So the real question is whether or not you will feel comfortable that we can meet our delivery commitments, is that right?"

Production prospective buyer: "Yes, that's it exactly."

Salesperson: "What kind of delivery do you expect?"

Production prospective buyer: "Within two days of our placing an order."

Salesperson: "OK. Do you have any other concerns about dealing with us?"

Production prospective buyer: "Only that research can assure us it meets our specifications."

Salesperson: "What other things will you consider when you are ready to make the decision about using our product?"

Note: At this point, the prospective buyer might give several points. Some examples are: price, company reputation, packaging. Or the buyer might say that he/she hasn't really thought about it beyond the concerns expressed. The salesperson can now suggest some things that are American Chemical strengths. One example would be their ability to respond to potential problems quickly because a technical support person will be assigned to the account full time for the first month the product is in production. This is a company strength that makes it more difficult for the competitor who can't offer it.

Salesperson: "Don't you think that is an important consideration?"

Production prospective buyer: "Yes, it is."

Salesperson: "If we could assure you that we can consistently deliver on schedule, that our product meets spec, does it consistently from batch to batch and will integrate into your production system easily, and we satisfy those other factors you

will take into account when making your decision, would you recommend us to be your supplier?"
Production prospective buyer: "Yes, I would."

The salesperson can now gear benefit statements to exactly how American Chemical can address those concerns, the basis for production's buying decision. One American Chemical Example would be:

Salesperson: "We have warehouses located in five major U.S. cities. One is in... only 400 miles from your facility. We can ship product to you over night, which would actually exceed your expectations. How does that sound?"
Production prospective buyer: "That sounds just fine."

The same process should take place for American Chemical's final two decision groups:
Marketing (and sales). Does this product have some advantages we can stress to our customers and will they receive a better end product?
Purchasing. Will the product be delivered on time to specification and are the terms and pricing competitive?
You should have noticed several things in the production prospective buyer scenario. The salesperson

1. asked questions (some were obviously commitment questions).
2. answered questions with questions.
3. followed up benefits statements with a trial close.
4. didn't state the benefit until it had been determined that the need for the benefit was important to the prospective buyer.

This last point is critical. Most salespeople simply tell their entire story. American Chemical's salespeople used to talk about the warehouses whether it was important to the prospective buyer or not, along with other benefits in what amounted to a monologue. They didn't determine in advance if they were important to the prospective buyer nor did they confirm that the benefits were important by trial closing. The prospective buyer was not involved. A benefit is only important if the prospective buyer needs it. Otherwise, it is not a benefit. Benefits must address prospective buyer concerns and the basis for the buying decision.
Selling to prospective buyer needs has not been mentioned and the reason is simple. Prospective buyers may know what their needs are but it's more difficult to ask them "what they need" than "what their

concerns are." If salespeople uncover prospective buyer concerns, they can determine what the prospective buyer needs.

In the scenario, the American Chemical salesperson made none of these mistakes with the production prospective buyer. Your salespeople must avoid these same mistakes by employing the techniques discussed.

Previously, you developed a value oriented opening statement that addressed typical prospective buyer concerns. List your typical prospective buyer concerns along with one or more benefits your company offers (either company, service, support or product related) that addresses each concern:

Concern: _____
Benefit: _____
Concern: _____
Benefit: _____
Concern: _____
Benefit: _____
Concern: _____
Benefit: _____
Concern: _____
Benefit: _____
Concern: _____
Benefit: _____

Ensure your salespeople use these benefits only after prospective buyer concerns and the basis for the buying decision have been determined.

Gain Appropriate Commitments

The American Chemical salesperson has gained commitments throughout the qualifying process. It is appropriate to ask now for the final commitment, "If research and production testing are successful and you are convinced we can address your other concerns, is there any reason why you wouldn't select us to be your supplier?" This question should be asked every time. It is essential to take the prospective buyer's temperature at this point—to find out where you stand. If there is any reason why he/she wouldn't select American Chemical, this is the place to find that out, not at the end of the funnel when most often it is too late. Again, if the response is a "No" or "I'm not sure," the salesperson can probe for the reasons why and respond accordingly.

Establish a Written Agenda

A written agenda for the balance of the steps confirms what the salesperson and prospective buyer have agreed will happen to make the sale. It is necessary for longer sales cycles and when multiple decision people are involved. If it's not in writing, the prospective buyer may think one thing while the salesperson thinks quite another. Even though it was verbally agreed to, time has a strange way of making people forget. If it's in writing, that won't happen.

Identify a Coach

A coach is most helpful. A coach is defined as someone in the prospective buyer organization who can help you avoid "land mines"—"land mines" being situations that could hurt your selling effort. One might be that the present supplier is making an attempt to reinforce its position. In the American Chemical example, they might make an attempt to straighten out the "testing" problem. It's important that the salesperson knows about it. The coach shouldn't sell for you but rather keep you informed of any situation that could hurt your effort.

The Next Step

Identify the next step and its objective at this point. Even though you and your prospective buyer have agreed on the steps to the sale, establish the next step and the objective for that next step after concluding each step.

American Chemical will submit a product for testing in the research lab. There are two objectives for that step: to complete the testing by an agreed-upon date, and to provide technical assistance as needed. It is important to confirm the next step and agree on its objective(s).

Chapter Summary

This completes the qualifying portion of the funnel. It is the step that requires a great amount of sales skill and focus. It takes a much shorter amount of time than the balance of the steps but sets the stage for the success or failure of each of those steps. It makes no sense to go from one step to the next without being sure the last step was performed to standard.

The qualifying elements discussed in this chapter become your performance standards for this step. If your salespeople haven't done each element and gotten the information you need to continue with the sale, have them go back and get it before proceeding to the next step. When coaching salespeople to perform the job to standard, make sure they can use these techniques. Then, observe them being used in live selling situations. Each of these issues is discussed in subsequent chapters.

Finally, I would like to give you an example that shows the futility of going through the entire sales process without qualifying. I received a telephone call from a home window company trying to sell me new windows. The telephone salesperson used a script that was very poorly written and had no qualifying questions. The salesperson did ask me what kind of windows I had but I didn't know how to answer that silly question—what did the salesperson want to know and why? The scripted presentation continued for five full minutes, which is a very long time if you are simply listening. At the end of this monologue, which I had allowed to continue because I am always interested in how salespeople present themselves, I was asked, "Would it be possible for me to set an appointment with you and Mrs. Frye to have one of our outside sales representatives come by and show you both the advantages of our windows?" Now, I could have agreed and put this company through the entire sales process, but I didn't want to play that game. So I explained to the salesperson that, in the first place, there was no Mrs. Frye and, in the second place, I rent and couldn't buy these windows even if I never had to pay a heating bill again. The salesperson said, "Oh, OK," and hung up.

It was a very unprofessional sales call to say the least. The major point is that they were willing to invest time and money into a hopeless situation. It happens all the time.

Chapter 4
The Balance of the Funnel Steps

The activities at each step of the remainder of American Chemical and other types of selling companies' activities follow. After each step is presented and discussed, you will develop the activities you want to be sure are done for your same step if you have one. You may have it under a different step number (for example ABC Software would give a presentation at Step 4 and a demonstration at Step 5, while American Chemical's demonstrations occur at Step 3 and Step 7 and presentation at Step 6).

American Chemical Step 3—Submit a Product for Testing

American Chemical must first have their product approved. It has to meet the prospective buyer's specifications. This is a product demonstration, that is, it will prove that the product will perform the way American Chemical said it would. The activities their salespeople must perform are:

1. Establish a schedule for the test. They don't want it put on the back burner or to drag on.
2. Gain agreement on what will be done should the product fail during testing. They don't want it to be a one-shot program.
3. Offer technical support. They don't want the test to fail because research didn't understand some specifics about the product properties.
4. Suggest some unique product properties that might make it superior to the current competitive product(s). They want to be sure research won't miss them.

Figure 4.1
The American Chemical Sales Funnel—Step 3

Newton's Steps 1 to 5

Newton Oriental Rug Fair which sells oriental rugs through retail stores has different steps 1 and 3. Figure 4.2 shows that their Step 1 is to advertise their store and products and Step 3 consists of the following:

1. Presentation

- Company presentation and its services
- The specifics of various types of oriental rugs and their relative values
- specific features and benefits of the rug(s) a prospective buyer likes

2. Showing rugs

- Many prospective buyers have an idea about what style and color oriental rug they would like. The salespeople have stacks of rugs about three to four feet high Each stack represents a different rug size (9' x 9', 8' x 10', etc.).

Figure 4.2
The Newton Oriental Rug Fair Sales Funnel—Step 8

THE MARKET

Step 1
Define the Best Prospective Buyers
Through Advertising and Word of Mouth

Step 2
Qualify
Those Coming into Stores

Step 3
Presentation—Show Rugs

Step 4
Close

Step 5
Product Home Trial

Step 6
Follow-up on Trial

Step 7
Close

Step 8
Follow-up

- The salespeople go through the rugs (by pulling back one corner of each) in the size requested until the prospective buyer spots one or perhaps two or three that seem to be right. Those rugs are then removed from the stacks and laid on the floor so the prospective buyer can see their full size next to one another.

Figure 4.3
The American Chemical Sales Funnel—Step 4

- After a few minutes, one of the three rugs is invariably eliminated. The prospective buyer normally looks from one to the other of the two remaining several times, thinking about who knows what. The salesperson, after a few minutes, will say: "You are probably not ready to make a decision today, I know, but if you were going to, which of these 2 rugs do you think you would take home?"

Invariably the prospective buyer will pick one of them. The salesperson will then go to step 4. If the close is unsuccessful, the salesperson goes to step 5, a trial in the home, to which the prospective buyer will agree in a large percentage of selling situations. The salespeople ask how long the prospective buyer will need to make the decision—they stipulate that it should be no longer than two days—they don't want any more time to go by before a decision is made. Then, they ask for a charge card or check that they will not process until a decision is made. It is torn up if the prospective buyer decides not to buy the rug.

Product Testing

If you have a step that requires a product test or a product trial, list the activities you expect your salespeople to perform at that step in the spaces provided:

1. _____
2. _____
3. _____
4. _____
5. _____
6. _____
7. _____
8. _____

American Chemical Step 4—Follow-up on the Testing

This is a critical step in American Chemical's funnel. (See Figure 4.3) Several things can go wrong at step 3:

1. The product might fail.
2. Competition might solve the batch-testing problem.
3. The test could be given a lower priority and not completed when American Chemical expects that it will. Even though a written agenda and testing schedule were agreed to, something might come along to change it. It can't be left to chance.
4. A new decision influencer could enter the picture with loyalties to the current supplier(s) or have some prejudices against American Chemical.

American Chemical performs the following activities at this step:

1. Contact the research person responsible for testing time frame: weekly
2. Contact the coach to see if everything is still on track or if anything has changed. Let the Coach know if testing is not on schedule and ask for suggestions to get it back on schedule. Time frame: weekly
3. Contact other decision people to

   • let them know if testing is off schedule and stress the urgency to stick to the schedule by restating business benefits to the company and personal benefits to the decision people.

- Keep them informed of the status of the testing and successes achieved along the way.
- Reconfirm the commitments already established— "if the test is successful, are we set for the production test" and "assuming we address all of your concerns, has anything new come up that would prevent you from selecting us (or recommending us) as your supplier?"

4. Send appropriate articles (American Chemical's or industry related) that support American Chemical's position in the marketplace, product performance in other companies, technological superiority, etc. Time frame: biweekly
5. Send materials related to supporting American Chemical's statements about their company, support capabilities, or product. These add to the credibility of both the salesperson and the company, indicate their interest informing and educating the prospective buyer and keeps American Chemical's name before the decision people. This is a very important activity. Time frame: as appropriate.

Salespeople should educate prospective buyers on issues about which they may be unaware. It further establishes credibility and prospective buyers are impressed.

At Newton Oriental Rug Fair, the educational process is done at Step 3—the specifics of various types of oriental rugs and their relative values (see figure 4.3). People who are uneducated about oriental rugs have difficulty understanding why one is more or less expensive than another (sometimes a significant difference in price). Or they may have thought about buying a machine-made oriental rug and Newton Oriental only sells hand made rugs. Their salespeople educate the prospective buyer about the way different rugs are made, the number of knots per square inch and why that is important, the kind of coloring agents used and why one may be better than another in certain situations, the value that a rug holds over the years and so on. It establishes both credibility and trust, a very important factor in any type of selling, retail or any other.

Newton's Step 6

Newton Oriental's Step # 6 is a follow-up to the product trial (see Figure 4.2). They telephone the prospective buyer after one to two days and ask the following:

- "How does the rug look in your living room?"
- "Do the colors go well with your furniture?"
- "Do you have any questions about the rug that I can answer for you?"
- "Please feel free to call me if you have any questions" They don't attempt a close at this point although the prospective buyer expects one. They wait until the next day to "close" on the telephone (Step 7).

If you have a follow-up step to product testing or a product trial, list the activities you expect your salespeople to perform at that step and/or what they should say in the spaces provided:

1. _____

2. _____

3. _____

4. _____

Surveys

As stated in Chapter 2, the purpose of a Survey is to determine the impact of your product on a prospective buyer's business financially. American Chemical in its Step 5 will contact the customer's research to perform several step activities, principally to determine if their product will improve performance in any financially quantifiable way. Their product will

- Provide better protection at extreme cold and warm driving conditions and at what degree levels (are they better than the current supplier?)
- Provide properties that make the engine run cleaner and by how much that could increase, for example, engine life
- Will make it easier for production to integrate and use their product on a regular basis and what it would mean to production (improve production throughput, reduce production failures and, therefore, rejection rates and by how much)

Figure 4.4
The American Chemical Sales Funnel—Step 5

Similarly they will contact customer's production and marketing, to make them aware of the quantifiable product impact discovered in testing to determine what the effect would be financially (increased sales, improved production scheduling, reduced rejection rates).

In addition, American Chemical knows that they can save the prospective buyer time and money by eliminating batch testing at the prospective buyer's site. Production can tell them how much time is spent on that function and the manpower costs associated. That savings alone might justify pricing differences with the competition.

In any event, this service is a measurable benefit for the prospective buyer.

Figure 4.5 shows the Intrepid Insurance Agency sales funnel. Their Step 4 is a survey although it is different in nature from American Chemical's survey. They need to know the following:

Figure 4.5
The Intrepid Insurance Agency Sales Funnel

THE MARKET

Step 1
Advertise to Define the Best Prospective Buyers

Step 2
Qualify
Only the Most Qualified Go to Step 3

Step 3
Sales Presentation

Step 4
Survey Prospective Buyer

Step 5
Proposal Preparation and Presentation

Step 6
Write the Order

Step 7
Delliver and Review Policy

Step 8
Account Management

Figure 4.6
The American Chemical Sales Funnel—Step 6

1. What risks to property, employees and visitors exist (which the prospective buyer may not know about)
2. The potential losses to be incurred if something catastrophic or a more minor incident were to happen
3. The value of the property—all assets

4.	The types of coverage the prospective buyer presently has, whether it would really cover all potential risks and the out-of-pocket expense the prospective buyer could have as a result

Presentations and Demonstrations

American Chemical's Step 6 calls for a formal presentation to all decision people (geared to concerns and the basis for the buying decision). Both the sales presentation and sales demonstration will be discussed in this step since American Chemical's demonstration can only be conducted in research and production testing where the salesperson is not in attendance. The product must perform pretty much on its own.

Typically, a product demonstration involves a salesperson, and, at times, one or more people from his/her company, and one or more people from the prospective buyer organization and is conducted either at the home office, the prospective buyer's office or at a user location. ABC Software conducts this type of demonstration. Examples of their demonstration activities will be given.

If you have both a presentation and demonstration in different funnel steps, simply use the strategies presented here in those steps.

The Presentation

Chapter 2 stated that a presentation is needed when one or more decision people want to hear about your company, its support service and product(s) simultaneously, and when your company, support services and product(s) cannot be demonstrated. For example, there is no way to prove that an advertising agency will provide the kinds of service a client expects. Samples of previous work can be seen and references provided but they don't prove what will be done for this client. It only creates a perception of what will be done.

The presentation should be designed to create the perception that your company, support services and products will meet the prospective buyer's concerns and the basis for the buying decision. It should also precede the demonstration, since a demonstration should support the claims made in the presentation.

Salespeople are ready for a presentation when they:

1.	have completed the survey (if one is needed) and verified findings with the decision people. If they aren't verified, they could be challenged during the presentation and thrown completely off course.

2.	have established a good working relationship with the decision person or people. This reinforces the need to talk to each of them early in the sales process.
3.	can ensure that all decision people will attend the presentation.
4.	have prepared visual selling aids such as:

- Presentation books
- Sound-slide presentations
- Video cassettes or film presentations
- Overhead transparencies
- Brochures
- Various exhibits (samples, forms, ads, etc.)
- Technical support material (spec sheets, etc.)

One or more of the selling aids may be used during the presentation to reinforce your sales points (also called benefits). Visually supporting sales points lends credibility to the entire message. Newton Oriental Rug fair does this by showing the number of knots per square inch and having the prospective buyer feel the difference between rugs with more and less knots per square inch. If you will use visual aids in your sales presentations, consider where they best fit in the four presentation steps you should follow. They are the attention, interest, conviction and decision steps.

The Attention Step. The purpose of this step is to get the audience's undivided attention and involve them in the presentation by making attention-getting statements and asking questions.

Salesperson: "Our survey of your operation shows that you could save as much as $ _____ per year by using American Chemical products as well as improve product performance. My purpose here today is to explain just how we can do that. If we can, is there any reason why you wouldn't go along with our program?"

The salesperson knows the concerns of each audience member but still takes their temperature to ensure nothing new has come up. If one of more new issues have come up, they must be addressed in the presentation, if at all possible. At the very least, the salesperson must know about them at this point so they can be addressed at a later date, if additional research or technical information is required. The sale could be lost, however, if they are not known.

The Interest Step. The purpose of this step is to address each of the concerns and the basis for the buying decision the participants raised in previous meetings.

Salesperson: "It's important that this presentation address your primary concerns about doing business with American

Chemical and what we can offer both you and your company. Let me begin by reviewing what you have told me is important to each of you. Mr. _____ of production is concerned about easily integrating our product into your operation, providing consistent quality and meeting your delivery requirements, is that right? (Yes) Is there anything else you would like me to address here? (No) Fine. Ms. _____ of purchasing wants to be sure..."

Salespeople should continue with each of the audience members in the same way, gaining agreement at the end of their concerns and other issues review. When they have completed this task, they should finish by saying, "The balance of this presentation will be geared to those critical issues we've just reviewed."

The Conviction Step. The purpose of this step is to present sales points that have been prepared to address all concerns and the bases for the buying decision. Sales points are benefit statements and form the core of the presentation. Sales points consist of:

1. a feature or fact about your company, support services and product. For example, the location of American Chemical's warehouses is a feature, a fact about the company.
2. the function of that feature—what it provides or how it works. In American Chemical's case, the warehouses are strategically located across the United States so that deliveries can be expedited.
3. the benefit—the value it provides a prospective buyer from either a business or personal point of view. As you recall, American Chemical's prospective buyer will benefit by getting deliveries overnight, faster than they expect to get them.

Many salespeople confuse functions and benefits and give the function only:

Salesperson: "We have warehouses located strategically across the country. One is located in _____, only a few hundred miles from your facility."

That statement doesn't address the prospective buyer's concerns— how fast can American Chemical deliver, not where their warehouses are located. The benefit must address the prospective buyer's concerns or it isn't a benefit. Be sure you and your salespeople understand this important difference.

After each sales point is made, it must be followed by a trial close: "You can see that will ensure you have product when you need it, wouldn't you agree?" Be sure you and your salespeople do this as well. Once all sales points have been made, the salesperson should go to the next presentation step.

The Decision Step. The purpose of this step is to make the decision people want to make the buying decision now.

> Salesperson, "So in review, we can offer your company (restate major benefits quickly). You agreed that if we did that, you would want to do business with American Chemical. Is there any reason why we shouldn't go ahead with the program now?"

The salesperson knows that, in this case, a trial production run must still occur. However, this question eliminates all other obstacles if it is answered affirmatively. If it is not, the salesperson needs to know it.

Remember the old adage—"Tell them what you're going to tell them, tell them, then tell them what you've told them." That is what should happen in the ideal presentation, finishing with the decision step. That is what happened in the four presentation steps.

The Demonstration

A selling demonstration is intended to prove that your product will do what your salespeople have said it will do. ABC Software will be used to illustrate how a selling demonstration should be conducted. It is a more typical product selling demonstration than American Chemical's research and production testing demonstrations.

ABC Software's demonstration step is Step 4. (See Figure 4.7) It follows qualifying (Step 2) and a presentation (Step 3). Since I am switching companies in mid-stream to illustrate the most common type of demonstration, it's appropriate to show ABC Software's funnel steps and where the demonstration step is done.

In addition to ABC Software's selling demonstration, they give two other types of demonstrations that should be discussed.

Product Awareness Demonstration. The purpose of this demonstration is to make potential prospective buyers interested in learning more about the product in a general sense. They are either unaware that a product like ABC Software's exists or are aware one exists but don't know much about it.

These demonstrations are typically given at trade shows and open houses. Open houses are often conducted by ABC Software either at their home office or hotels in strategic locations around the country.

Potential prospective buyers are invited to attend by their salespeople. These demonstrations are often on videotape or film, although ABC personnel usually do them.

They are given to relatively large groups (5 to 20 people) where the types of work flow the prospective buyers perform, typical business and personal concerns, and other qualifying data are not known. They are designed to create sufficient interest in the product so

Figure 4.7
The ABC Software Sales Funnel

prospective buyers will want a "personalized" demonstration—a selling demonstration.

This type of demonstration should last 10 minutes or less. If it goes longer than that, two negative things can happen. *First*, the attendees can lose interest and attention. ABC Software used to show one participant how certain things were done on the system in detail, which didn't interest many of the others. Second, the system may not appear easy to use. It can appear to be hard to use, which will turn prospective buyers off.

This type of demonstration should focus on business and personal benefits that can be derived from sharing data and the types of data that can be shared. If it becomes overly technical, that emphasis can be lost.

Installation Demonstrations. As the name implies, this demonstration will be given once the purchase has been made and either before or when the system or product is delivered and installed. It is often given before delivery so that customer personnel will be able to use it upon delivery.

These last two types of demonstrations are mentioned not only because they are important but also because they are sometimes confused with the selling demonstration. Neither of them will sell the product because they aren't meant to prove that the product will do exactly what the prospective buyer wants it to do.

The Selling Demonstration. This demonstration is designed to get the order if it proves the product will do what the prospective buyer wants it to do. To maximize the chances of this happening, your salespeople should do what ABC Software's salespeople do:

1. Restate the prospective buyer's concerns and basis for the buying decision. They then gain agreement with trial closes.
2. Plan and present sales points that will be both stated and shown during the demonstration and geared to those concerns and basis for the buying decision.
3. Summarize the sales points and ask for the buying decision.

ABC Software does several things before, during and after the demonstration. You should do the same.

Before the selling demonstration. There are four concerns of the ABC salespeople before the selling demonstration. *First*, they prepare and practice the demonstration. Many selling demonstrations have been ruined because this wasn't done. It is especially important when the plan is for a technical support person to physically run the product while the salesperson describes what is happening. They must be in "sync."

Compelling Vision, Inc. sells computers to newspapers with software that allows the newspaper to make up entire pages on one screen so, for example, editors can see the layout and decide if certain stories should be moved and/or replaced by other more important stories. On one particular demonstration, the salesperson had not told the technical support person what the prospective buyer's particular interest and concerns were and, believe it or not, actually left the demonstration room during the demonstration. The prospective buyer didn't see what he expected to see and the sale was lost.

It doesn't matter whether it's Compelling Vision, a copier/facsimile dealer, a computer retail store, a medical company selling X-ray equipment to dentists or IBM. Prospective buyers had better see what they expect to see in the demonstration and agree that they have seen it and like it.

Second, ABC Software checks out the system to ensure that it is working properly. If your salespeople are trying to prove the product will do what they have said it will do and it malfunctions, it raises the question that if they can't make it work in an ideal situation what will happen in a production situation. I can't remember how many times I have seen this happen. One of my clients is a facsimile dealer. (See Figure 4.8) Their salespeople carry a facsimile unit in their car and put it on a dolly to make it easy to take to various office buildings. They call on every small business with one decision person in that building and look for opportunities to demonstrate the machine.

On too many occasions, the salespeople would plug the facsimile unit in, turn it on and try to send a prospective buyer document to their office facsimile number to show how fast and easy it is to use their system. But the document wouldn't send. The salespeople would then say something like: "Well, something is wrong but that's because this is a demonstration unit and has been taken around in my car for several weeks and used many times in demonstrations like this. A new machine wouldn't have this problem."

This statement tells the prospective buyer that this facsimile machine won't stand up to heavy use. Their salespeople are trying to make the best of a bad situation but, in fact, only make it worse. Consequently, we added a step in their sales funnel (see Figure 4.8) that requires each salesperson to test the equipment each morning before going on the road by sending a document to and receiving one from the office. We also added a scripted statement about what to say if the product should fail during the demonstration.

Third, if a technical support person is to run the equipment, ABC Software makes sure that person knows what the prospective buyer expects to see and why it is important to address the concerns and the

Figure 4.8
Facsimile Dealer Sales Funnel

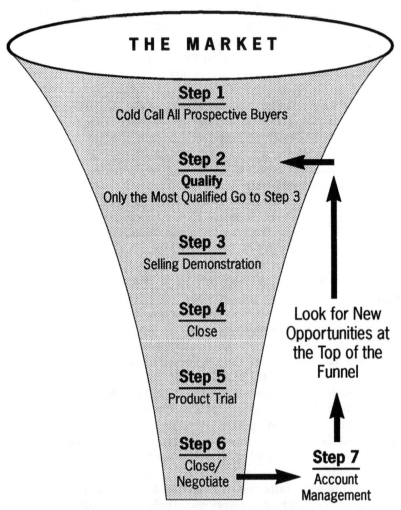

prospective buyer. If this isn't done, the technical support person may show the prospect something that is a turn off.

At one demonstration, the ABC Software technical person explained each keystroke in detail to a prospective buyer who wanted to see how fast and easy the system was to operate. Needless to say, the system appeared to be slow and difficult to use when in reality it is a very fast and easy-to-use system.

Fourth and finally, they get samples or examples of the prospective buyer's type of work. It is important to show how the product will do that work if at all possible. The worst scenario (which has happened all too often) is when the prospective buyer brings a particular application to the demonstration, asks to see how it is done and finds that it takes several minutes (or longer) to set up the product up to do it. It makes it seem difficult and time consuming, hardly the impression the salesperson wants to create. This used to happen to ABC Software's salespeople but it doesn't any longer. They get samples in advance of the Demonstration and prepare running the sample so the Demonstration will go smoothly at that point the prospective buyer expects to see it done.

During the Demonstration. There are eight basic steps that ABC Software follow during the demonstration. They are enumerated here.

1. ABC Software's salespeople get the amenities out of the way— things like introductions, a facilities tour if appropriate, etc.

2. They then sit the prospective buyer(s) down away from the product (in an office or conference room) and review each concern and basis for the buying decision. This: a) reestablishes why they are there and what they expect to see, b) lets their salespeople know if there have been any changes in or additions to these major issues, and c) allows their salespeople to gain and maintain control of the demonstration.

Since they will establish what the prospective buyers expect to see, they can prevent irrelevant prospective buyer questions from interfering with the flow of the demonstration. Prospective buyers often ask questions like, "What is that?" or "Why did it do this?" or "How does that work?" If your salesperson responds, the demonstration can become sidetracked. Typically, after answering one question and showing it on the product, another question "pops" into the prospective buyer's mind. This can go on and on and ruin a demonstration.

If the question is relevant but a response would be distracting, their salespeople say, "It's interesting you should ask that because I had planned to cover it in just a few minutes. Is it OK if we hold off for a bit?" If the prospective buyer persists, your salespeople may have to explain it but must get back on track as soon as possible.

3. They then ask the commitment question, "If you see how ABC Software can help you meet your objectives and address all the issues on the table today, is there any reason why we couldn't finalize the decision today?"

The commitment question must be asked. If there is any reason why the prospective buyer(s) would not make the decision today, it's essential to determine why and proceed from there. Why go through the entire demonstration if there are other issues to be addressed?

4. ABC Software's salespeople watch for prospective buyer reactions and buying signals so control is maintained. For example, if a prospective buyer looks away or whispers something to an associate, ask, "Is there something that needs clarification?" If the prospective buyer gives a buying signal like, "My people should be able to make that work easily," respond by saying "Can you see how quickly you can be up and running productively in a short period of time?" (a trial close)

5. They use trial closes after each sales point—"Having that data shared by your sales and sales management people will be a significant improvement over your present system, wouldn't you agree?" If they get yeses, they continue. If not, they stop and find out why. As has been stated many times in this chapter, your salespeople must constantly take the prospective buyer's temperature to be sure the sale is on track by having the prospective buyer agree with each sales point. That is what ABC Software's salespeople do.

6. ABC Software involves the prospective buyer in the demonstration physically as well as verbally. They have the prospective buyer operate parts of the demonstration that are relatively easy to do to reinforce that very point. Unless your product is so complicated that it can't be done, let prospective buyers do some parts of the demonstration.

7. They don't overdo technical jargon. ABC Software won't talk about bits and bytes and programming language. They can confuse a prospective buyer. Technical people might be interested in those issues but they don't make the final buying decision. A typical decision person will want to see things like:

a) How easy the system is to operate
b) Its speed
c) How fast it performs certain types of applications
d) What customer, prospective buyer, sales calls, proposals delivered, sales made and other pertinent sales and marketing related information is available

These are the things to be demonstrated. If someone asks you for the time, they are not interested in how the watch was built. If it is necessary to go into technical details with technical people, do it at a later time. This is a selling demonstration, not a technical discussion.

8. There are many dead spots in ABC Software's demonstration. Their product delays for one to two minutes for certain pieces of information to be sorted before appearing on the screen. One to two minutes may not seem like a long time but is an eternity if everyone is staring at a blank screen. It clearly makes the product seem slow.

ABC Software plans what will be said during the dead spots. Your salespeople should do the same if you have that kind of situation.

The facsimile dealer's salespeople have to describe certain features and benefits of their system while it is transmitting a document. Otherwise, everyone involved will stand there in silence watching a piece of paper feed into the machine. A minute takes a long time if no one is saying anything.

After the Selling Demonstration. ABC salespeople sit the prospective buyer(s) down once again away from the product and do what was done at the end of the presentation:

Salesperson: "Let's review what we have just done (restates the major benefits and gains agreement that they will help meet prospective buyer objectives). You agreed that if we met those objectives, there wouldn't be any reason not to go ahead with the decision today (the commitment question restated). Why don't we finalize the details now?" (This is a close and will be discussed in detail at that step in the process.)

Presentation and demonstration were both presented in Step 6 although they will each typically be in different steps. The real issue is to ensure that your salespeople follow the rules for giving effective presentations and demonstrations and utilize commitment questions and trial closes throughout each of them.

American Chemical Steps 7 and 8—Perform a Trial Production Run and Follow-up

Agreement for this Step 7 was made early in the process (Step 2). American Chemical delivers the product to the production person responsible for the testing. They used to ship it but determined that the agreed-upon testing schedule wasn't always adhered to (even if it was discussed on the phone). They find that it is more likely to be followed if reaffirmed in a face-to-face meeting.

This is particularly important in production testing because it means the production line has to be shut down long enough to run the tests in almost every case, which is a major reason for production testing delays—production can't seem to "find the time." Typically, American Chemical's Production tests can be run in one to two days.

If a production test is one of your funnel steps, your salespeople must be sure production is committed to do it according to the schedule. American Chemical also repeats the offer of technical assistance as needed.

As was the case in Step 4, American Chemical's step 8, follow-up is critical in their funnel. The same kind of things can go wrong as in Step 7:

Figure 4.9
The American Chemical Sales Funnel—Step 7

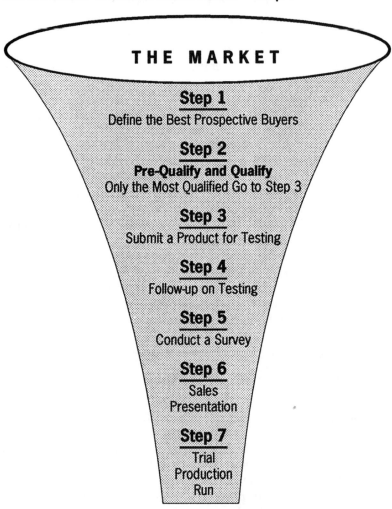

THE MARKET

Step 1
Define the Best Prospective Buyers

Step 2
Pre-Qualify and Qualify
Only the Most Qualified Go to Step 3

Step 3
Submit a Product for Testing

Step 4
Follow-up on Testing

Step 5
Conduct a Survey

Step 6
Sales
Presentation

Step 7
Trial
Production
Run

1. The product might fail.
2. Competition might solve the batch testing problem.
3. The test could be interrupted because they need to get back to the production schedule.
4. A new decision influencer could enter the picture with loyalties to the current supplier(s) or have some prejudices against American Chemical.

Figure 4.10
The American Chemical Sales Funnel—Step 8

American Chemical performs contacting activities at this step: They contact the production person responsible for testing (time frame: every two days), and, contact the coach to see if everything is still on track or if anything has changed—let the coach know if testing is not on schedule and ask for suggestions to get it back on schedule. They also contact other decision people to:

- let them know if testing is off schedule and stress the urgency to stick to the schedule by restating

business benefits to the company and personal benefits to the decision people.
- keep them informed of the status of the testing and successes achieved along the way.
- reconfirm the commitments already established— "Assuming we address all of your concerns, has anything new come up that would prevent you from selecting us (or recommending us) as your supplier?"

The time frame for this contact activity is once every three days if the tests haven't been completed.

Other Follow-ups

Travcorps, Inc., the traveling nurse company described in Chapter 3 has a different follow-up schedule from that of American Chemical. (See Figure 4.11). After receiving a call from a nurse inquiring about working with Travcorps, the salesperson will follow-up in two weeks if the application was not received (Step 4).

They will wait two more weeks and follow up once again if the application was not received. If the application has been received, they state that and describe the rest of the application and pre-assignment process, which includes reference checking, acceptance into the program, matching assignments to the nurse's wishes.

Before their sales funnel was developed, Travcorp's salespeople would perform these functions at random times, or not follow up at all. Their selling system now has controls and their management can make certain the steps occur as they are supposed to occur. It has increased the number of nurses they have added to their program as measured against those prior to developing the sales funnel.

If you have a follow-up step to product testing step, any other step, or multiple follow-up steps as in Travcorp's case, list the activities you expect your salespeople to perform in the spaces provided:

1. _____
2. _____
3. _____
4. _____
5. _____
6. _____
7. _____

Figure 4.11
The Travcorps Sales Funnel—Step 8

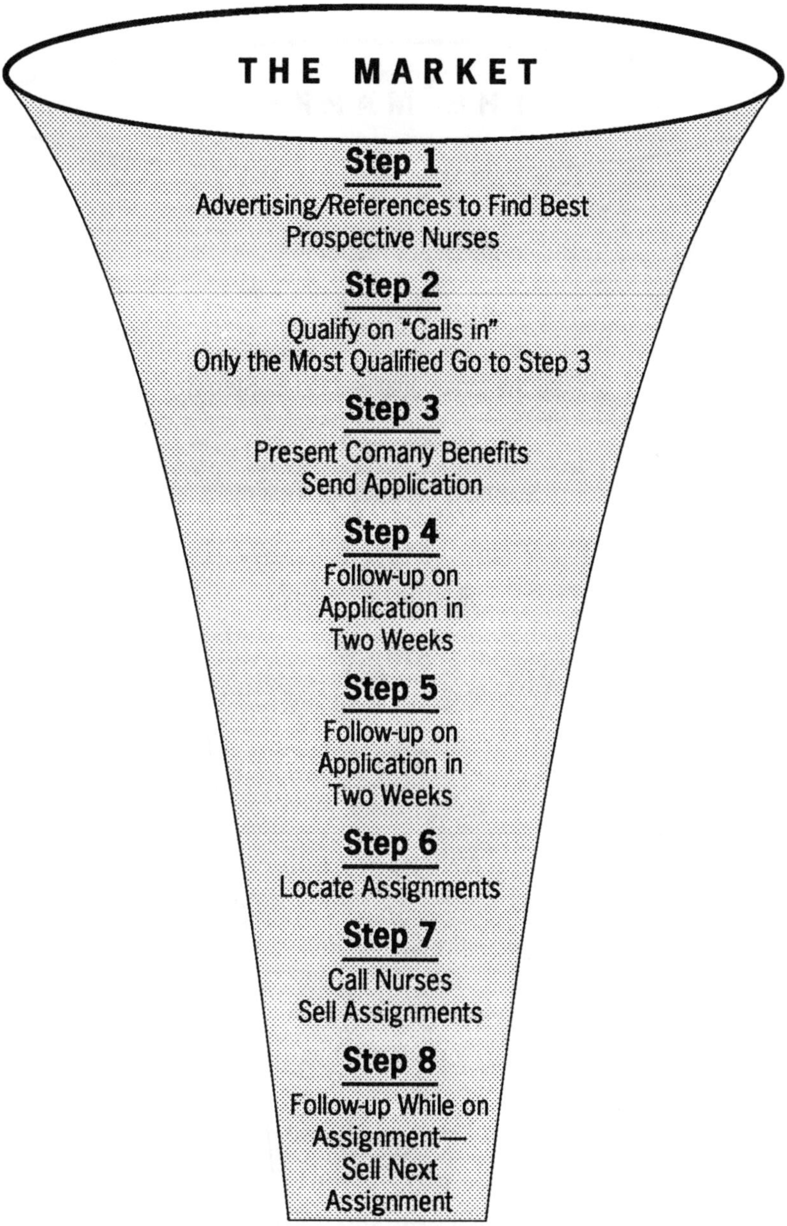

THE MARKET

Step 1
Advertising/References to Find Best
Prospective Nurses

Step 2
Qualify on "Calls in"
Only the Most Qualified Go to Step 3

Step 3
Present Comany Benefits
Send Application

Step 4
Follow-up on
Application in
Two Weeks

Step 5
Follow-up on
Application in
Two Weeks

Step 6
Locate Assignments

Step 7
Call Nurses
Sell Assignments

Step 8
Follow-up While on
Assignment—
Sell Next
Assignment

Figure 4.12
The American Chemical Sales Funnel—Step 9

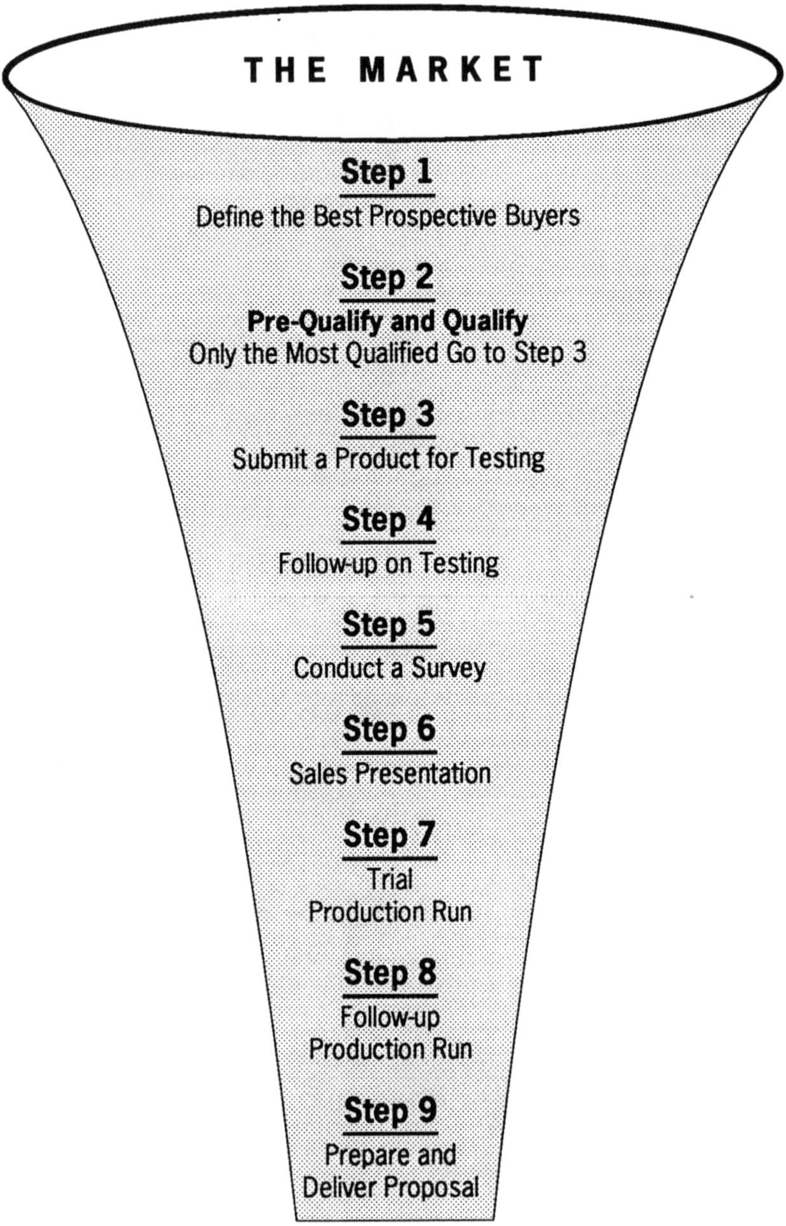

THE MARKET

Step 1
Define the Best Prospective Buyers

Step 2
Pre-Qualify and Qualify
Only the Most Qualified Go to Step 3

Step 3
Submit a Product for Testing

Step 4
Follow-up on Testing

Step 5
Conduct a Survey

Step 6
Sales Presentation

Step 7
Trial
Production Run

Step 8
Follow-up
Production Run

Step 9
Prepare and
Deliver Proposal

Proposals

A proposal should continue to sell your product or service when your salespeople are not there. Since buying decisions are made for business and personal reasons, your proposal should address those specific reasons. (See Figure 4.12 which shows The American Chemical Sales Funnel—Step 9.)

Too often, a proposal is nothing more than a quotation—a statement of the items to be purchased and associated pricing. American Chemical used to submit "quotes," which created two problems. *First,* the decision influencers would make their recommendations to someone American Chemical might not have met (the vice president of operations, the vice president of finance, etc.). They reached the key decision people but not at the vice presidential levels, who generally rubber stamp recommendations but will ask questions about why American Chemical should be the supplier. If those reasons aren't stated in writing, the decision influencers must answer from memory and most likely won't remember all the value issues. It can be embarrassing.

Second, the decision may then be made on price—comparing American Chemical to the existing supplier. After the time and effort spent on an account, it would be unfortunate, to say the least, if the decision boiled down to price alone. This happens frequently.

If only a quote (a pricing schedule on one or two sheets of paper) is delivered, it could have been done without all the efforts made to sell this account the right way. That is "activity for activity's sake" and quotes don't sell anyone anything by themselves. A proposal can and does. American Chemical now arms the key decision contacts with all the information needed to justify the buying decision.

Their proposals continue to sell the product when they are not there. The proposal will be discussed in detail after the salespeople have left. Therefore, it must reinforce the business and personal reasons for making the buying decision (and making it now).

The major advantages of a selling proposal are:

1. It keeps the momentum going despite possible delays in the decision making process.
2. Key decision people will want to get the program going and push for it.
3. Primary contacts can put their names on the proposal and submit it as their recommendation. It enhances their position in the organization.

Proposal Elements

The proposal elements presented are what should be covered in each section of the written proposal, with examples where appropriate.

The Cover Letter. The cover letter should be addressed to the primary contact and should not be longer than one typewritten page. There are five elements of the cover letter:

1. Briefly thank the primary contact (and other key decision people) for providing information needed to prepare a proposal that meets the prospect's objectives.

2. State the business issues that were agreed to early in the sales process and that they will be met by accepting the proposal.

3. State the financial justification you have developed in summary form, "You can achieve savings of $ _____ in the first year alone." This number should hit them at the beginning for three reasons:
   a) It creates immediate interest in the balance of the proposal.
   b) They may not believe that number and want to challenge it. Since there will be a detailed justification page in the proposal, the degree of research and effort put into determining how the number was determined will impress them. c) It keeps people from jumping immediately to the pricing section to see how much the product costs. If that happens, they may not even bother with the balance of the proposal.

4. State how the proposal will be followed up (specific dates and actions).

5. American Chemical states that the product has met specifications in research tests and has met standards established by production. It then stresses their commitment to work with the prospect organization to ensure the business objectives are met.

Table of Contents. A table of contents (each proposal element) should be included in any formal, written Proposal.

Title Page. The title page should indicate that the proposal was tailored to the prospect. Here is an example:

Implementation of an Oil Additive Program
Prepared for: _____ (prospect company name)
Attention: _____ (primary contact's name)
Prepared by: _____ (American Chemical Company)
Date: _____

Statement of Objectives. State the prospect's business objectives in bulleted form. Here is an example:

(Company name) has five objectives that American Chemical must meet. They are:

1. Eliminate the need for (prospect company) to test every incoming oil additive batch, which is time consuming and costly
2. Meet delivery requirements
3. Provide sales and marketing advantages
4. Provide improved product performance
5. Provide consistent performance in production from batch to batch

These objectives are the concerns and basis for making the buying decision that were expressed early in the sales process. The objectives should be followed by this statement: "This proposal details how American Chemical will achieve the objectives"

Analysis of the Present Situation. Describe some of the problems the prospect faces today and the potential for problems if they exist. American Chemical stresses the problems associated with testing every incoming batch of the current oil additive product (time spent, how that time could be spent more productively and associated costs).

They would also state that even though delivery is not a problem today (the prospect expects and gets it in two days), improved delivery will decrease the potential for production delays due to product shortage (they can deliver it overnight).

Analysis of the present situation clearly shows that American Chemical has done their homework and understands the prospect's business issues. It establishes credibility and the perception that "they care about our situation."

Description of the Proposed Solution. American Chemical describes how they, their support services and the product will improve the business situation and achieve the objectives. It details, step-by-step, what they offer for each of the objectives listed on the objectives page—their solution for each one. This is a recap of the sales points made both in the presentation and demonstration and maintains continuity through the selling process.

Financial Justification. American Chemical provides detailed results of their survey and the associated financial impact on the prospect's organization. It is then totaled and obviously agrees with the dollar amount on the cover page.

Include a Completed Order Form. The objective is to get them to either sign it or attach it to the paperwork needed to create a purchase order.

Other Materials. American Chemical attaches product literature, specification details, industry articles, third-party reference letters, etc. that are relevant to the sale. This really becomes an appendix to the proposal and should be described as such.

Presenting the Proposal

There are several rules American Chemical follows when presenting a proposal. They:

1. Walk the primary contact through the proposal to ensure he/she understands and agrees with its contents.
2. Have the primary contact stay with their salesperson and not read ahead.
3. Determine if the recommended follow-up is the best course of action.
4. Try to gain a commitment for going ahead with the program.
5. Ask if the proposal will be reviewed by other people, determine if they can be there to present it and answer questions. This will ensure that the information is presented the way they want it presented. If the American Chemical salesperson is not permitted to be there, he/she schedules a meeting with the primary contact immediately after the proposal is reviewed by other decision people. It's important to find out if there are any problems or issues with the proposal or the program that could delay or cause a "No" decision as soon as possible.

Proposal Summary

Writing and presenting proposals can be a vital selling tool in all businesses. In my consulting business, I write very detailed proposals following the guidelines presented on the preceding pages. Acme Northeast's salespeople send quotes to prospective buyers either by facsimile or in the mail with no other information. Consequently, 75 percent of their follow-up telephone calls to those prospective buyers result in "your prices are too high." It's very difficult to regroup and make the sale at that point. It only works for Acme if the salespeople already know what the prospective buyer is paying and officially quote a lower price. But the sale has turned into a "price sell" only with no company or product benefits involved. That type of customer will give the next lowest bidder the business. No real business relationship has been established based on a professional presentation and proposal. We're going to change that at Acme.

Figure 4.13
The American Chemical Sales Funnel—Steps 10 and 11

One of my clients sells an environmental testing service to building owners and architects to name just two types of buyers. They are also in a highly competitive marketplace. The proposal helps separate them from their competition, helps establish their credibility, details the potential financial impact on building alterations if, for example, asbestos exists and how their services can detail what must be done to minimize the risks.

It may seem that it is too difficult and time consuming to write a detailed proposal on every sale. But much of it can be "boiler plate" material. That means that much of the information can be used from one proposal to another—only minimal changes need to be made. Several of my clients store the boiler plate material in a word processor or personal computer with a word processing program and only have to fill in the blanks and make other minor changes that significantly reduce proposal preparation time. Gathering the data is not the problem—typing a detailed proposal from scratch is the problem. Word processing minimizes it.

American Chemical Step 10—Follow Up

The cover letter described what follow up actions would take place, including a meeting scheduled right after the proposal review. It is critical to stick to them because delays can occur between the time the proposal is delivered and a decision is made, especially when several decision people must approve the sale. The excuses when delays occur are things like, "Jack is on vacation and won't be back for two weeks," or "The paperwork is stuck in purchasing."

It is the American Chemical salesperson's responsibility to manage the follow-up process with the coach's help and keep the sale moving. For example, other decision people can approve the program so that when Jack gets back from vacation, he will be the final approval person. Their salespeople contact purchasing to determine when they will approve it. The coach can help make it happen. These are strategic issues that must be discussed between you and your salespeople. American Chemical does it regularly. Salespeople typically wait until "Jack gets back" or "purchasing approves it" without taking any action to make it happen.

Follow-up at appropriate steps is as critical as any step in the sales process. It can mean the difference between getting the order now or getting it in six months or longer, which happens much too frequently in sales today. That is why it is so important to determine what the decision process is at the qualifying step. Your salespeople will know where the paperwork has to go, which will help them keep it moving.

Step 11—Close the Sale

Closing is not really a step in itself. Many commitment questions, trial closes and one closing question have been asked during the process. However, all step activities have been completed except for getting the order and it probably requires asking for it.

A trial close asks for an opinion. A closing question asks for a decision—something that many prospects are reluctant to make because it is stressful. As has been stated, people are reluctant to make decisions requiring change because it might be the wrong decision. Salespeople don't like to ask for the order because they are afraid the answer will be "No." So they wait for the prospect to order. That simply won't cut it.

American Chemical covered all the bases so far and now need the decision. There are several types of closes they use. Your salespeople should use them too. (See Figure 4.14)

Alternate Choice Close

Give the prospect a choice between two alternatives where the acceptance of either one means a buying decision has been made:

Salesperson: "Would you prefer the product packaged in 10 or 50 gallon drums?"

Either answer indicates that they are ready to buy—ask "I'll note that—when should we begin with the first shipment?"

List the types of things your salespeople could uses as alternates of choice in the spaces below:

1. _____ or _____

2. _____ or _____

3. _____ or _____

4. _____ or _____

Minor Point Close

Ask the primary contact to agree to some minor point that will confirm the buying decision:

Salesperson: "Will you issue a purchase order?"

Assumptive Close

Assume the primary contact is "ready to buy" and fill out the order form. If he/she doesn't stop you, you have the order.

Figure 4.14
The American Chemical Sales Funnel—Steps 11 and 12

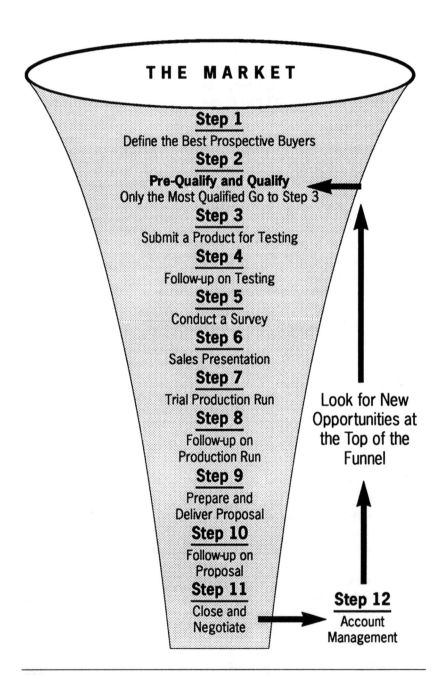

Straightforward Close

> Salesperson: "What do we have to do to finalize the program and get you started using our product?"

When a "close" is attempted, one of two things happens: the primary contact agrees to "buy," or an objection is raised. When an objection is raised at this step of the process, your salesperson's objective should be to make it the final one and close on it using the following six rules:

1. Listen to the objection all the way through. Nothing irritates like being interrupted. Prospects like salespeople who listen to them.
2. Agree with the prospect's right to feel the way he/she feels about it (don't agree with the objection—just the right to feel that way about it).
3. Restate the objection and expand on it. For example, if an American Chemical prospect says, "Your price is too high," the response is, "I understand how you feel. If I hear you correctly, you feel that the price isn't justified by the batch testing and other advantages we offer, is that right?"
    The prospect might say, "No, I guess it really is." (This, by the way, reinforces the need to sell value and how value can overcome price differentials.) The next rule describes what to do if the answer is, "Yes, that's right."
4. Question the objection, "May I ask why our pricing presents such a problem at this point?" The prospect will answer in some fashion.
5. Confirm that this is all that stands between you and the order. "So if it weren't for the pricing issue, you would have gone ahead with our program today, is that right?"
    If the prospect agrees, ask, "What do we have to do to overcome the problem?" If the prospect says, "No, there are some other issues as well," find out what they are. More selling is required.
6. If the answer is, "Reduce the price by 10 percent" and you can do it, confirm that you will and say, "I guess we're ready to go ahead with the program then."

Note: In this instance, negotiations are taking place. Basic negotiating strategies are discussed on the next page. The prospect says something like "I need to think it over for a few days." This is a stall, period! The decision is simply being avoided. The prospect typically won't spend one minute "thinking it over." The objective is to attempt to get the order now. This is a difficult situation for three reasons: a) Salespeople will walk away thinking the sale is safe or in the bag when it isn't; b) There is no real objection for salespeople to address head on; c) When they call the prospect at a later time, there is some excuse for not making the decision now and the process drags on, and on...

When your salespeople get the "I want to think this over for a few days," they should respond as follows: "I'm glad you want to think our program over. It means that you are really interested in our program (or product). Just to clarify my thinking, may I ask what part of our program you want to think over? Is it (restate each major benefit)?"

The prospect will likely respond with a "no" to each benefit because there really isn't anything to think over. At some point, an objection will be raised. All your salespeople have to do, then, is use the six rules for handling an objection and your chances of getting the order today are greatly increased.

This may sound like a "mind game" but it really isn't. Prospects will avoid making buying decisions by saying they "want to think it over for a few days." When your salesperson calls back in a few days, there is another excuse. This can go on for weeks! Salespeople must help prospects make the right decision. If buying your product or service is the right decision, your salespeople should use any reasonable technique to get that decision. Obviously, these techniques won't work in every case. But it is important that they be used in every case. They will increase your salespeople's closing percentages.

Negotiations

The primary objective in negotiations is to develop a "win-win" relationship with the prospect for several reasons:

1.   It establishes your salesperson and the prospect as partners in the process.
2.   It turns a potential "you-me" situation to a "we-our" relationship.
3.   It can reinforce your salespeople's integrity, which leads to greater credibility.
4.   It eliminates the adversarial relations that can result from negotiations. Even if the sale is made, one of the parties may feel the deal wasn't fair.

Many salespeople become anxious or defensive when a prospect asks for concessions on pricing, terms, warranties, training, technical support—more than what is normally allowed. Some salespeople have negotiating latitude but the great majority are constrained by company policies.

The real problem is that too many salespeople are afraid the sale is in jeopardy when concessions are requested. It may be, but in most cases it is not. In fact, the prospect has probably been sold but, as a negotiator, wants to see if a better arrangement can be made.

This fear causes salespeople to give the store away when it isn't necessary. As an example, a computer dealer's salesperson gave the price of a printer to American Chemical's manager of information services and immediately said, "I can probably get my manager to lower that price" without any prodding.

Using sound negotiating strategies will help your salespeople handle these situations professionally. There are training programs that deal specifically with negotiations. Most purchasing agents have attended one of them. Other decision people are good negotiators because they do it regularly and have the upper hand when a salesperson asks for the order. If negotiations are a problem for your salespeople, you may want to send them to one of these programs. What follows are simply guidelines for negotiation situations.

Negotiating Strategies

A review of why most negotiations are handled unsuccessfully sets the stage for the strategies to use. They are unsuccessful because:

1. Goals are not established before negotiations begin. Simply stated, your salespeople must know what your company's limits are.
2. Lack of preparation—your salespeople know what prospects typically ask for in negotiations. They must be prepared with your company's bottom line on each issue and what intermediate positions they can take (part way on issues). They should give away a little at a time and trial close after each one.
3. Not knowing the relative value of the negotiating points. Salespeople must know which are of greatest value to the prospect and which are of least value.
4. The desire to get it over quickly and get the order. Salespeople should take their time and not feel pressured to give away too much too fast.
5. It must be finished now. It *doesn't* have to be done now. The prospect may want some time to consider the situation, and it will take one or more additional calls to complete the negotiating process.
6. Fear of deadlocks. If agreement can't be reached and negotiations are broken off by the prospect, there is a fear that the sale is lost. Prospects typically respect a salesperson who doesn't cave in and continues to stress the value issues. It isn't

lost yet. Many sales have been won when the salesperson said, "I've done all I can do—you know you're getting real value with our product. I'm just sorry that we can't go ahead with the program today" and the prospect either said "OK" or, if the salesperson left, called to say "OK, let's do it."

With these issues in mind, what does a good negotiator do:

1. Uses good business judgment by thinking of the sale as if it affects his/her own business
2. Deals effectively with ambiguity or vague areas—doesn't see everything as black and white
3. Prepares for the negotiations with just what can be conceded and what cannot
4. Shows patience. Listens well. Lets the prospect's position unfold with real interest
5. Listens with an open mind. Doesn't let the "Oh boy, here we go again" defensive attitude creep into the discussion when the prospect asks for something
6. Gets all of the prospect's negotiating points out on the table at one time. Doesn't take one, agree to it, then another pops up and is agreed to, and so on, and so on...
7. Maintains control by asking questions and determining which of the issues really stands between us and going ahead with the program today
8. Makes the prospect feel like a partner in resolving the "issues that stand between us"
9. Avoids becoming argumentative, even if the prospect does
10. Remains calm when pressure is applied, even if the pressure is felt

Salespeople should prepare for negotiations by:

1. Listing every issue they expect to be raised from their experience
2. Determining which are:
   - Must haves
   - Nice to have
   - Will take it if it's offered but is not very important
3. Developing a summary of the benefits your company provides
4. Planning trades—"we will give something up if you give something up"

There are extensive courses available on negotiations. The points raised here are simply intended to offer guidelines for your salespeople. They take practice but can work for you if you help them stick to the rules.

Step 12—Provide Account Management

This is the last step in American Chemical's sales funnel. (See Figure 4.14.) It not only completes the process but sets the stage for additional business either with this department or division, or other departments or divisions within the company.

Account management can be described in these terms:

1. Ensuring the successful use of your products and services through effective internal training and management
2. Recommending new product and service upgrades
3. Maintaining an ongoing relationship with all key decision people within the organization
4. Gaining leads, references, market or product/service related intelligence
5. Maintaining account records

Less sophisticated salespeople refer to this as account maintenance that implies the objective is to maintain the status quo. The objective is to continue to look for selling opportunities. That is account management. Following are some techniques for account management:

1. Never make a sales call that does not include a selling objective (looking for new product or product upgrade opportunities, for example). Most customers don't like to have salespeople "drop in" or "call up" with no purpose in mind.
2. Ensure proper start-up. This may be where hand holding is needed. Help a customer through this transition and your salespeople will have a friend forever.
3. Monitor product application. Ensure that your products are providing the value the customer expects. If full utilization isn't realized, it opens the door to the competition.
4. Look for opportunities to sell by:
   - getting the names of other people (in this company or others) who might be interested in your products and services.
   - looking for new applications for your products and services.

- looking for upgrade potential (add-on capabilities).
5. Maintain an ongoing relationship at all levels.

Salespeople may not plan to see (or telephone) all key decision people on follow-on calls. It may seem that there is nothing to say to them. However, it's important to review the benefits and capabilities they are getting from your products and services.

Customer people will spread the word about your product's success if they're encouraged to do so. It's important to be sure they like your product—they can also spread the word about its lack of success as well.

Chapter Summary

American Chemical's step activities are completed with this chapter, which included ABC Software's demonstration step and a diagram of their funnel and other types of selling environments. Your similar steps should be done much the same way. If you should have one or more steps that were not included here, determine what activities must be performed at those steps. Most, if not all, have been covered however.

You now have the standards of performance for your salespeople at each of your steps. By monitoring performance at each step, you will be able to

1. identify objectively where a sale has gone wrong.
2. anticipate potential problems and head them off.
3. identify specific training requirements.
4. eliminate activity for activity's sake.
5. do several other important sales management functions that are detailed in subsequent chapters.

As has been said many times, the purpose of the sales funnel is to ensure your salespeople do what they are supposed to do when they are supposed to do it. A close friend of mine owns and operates a country store where one can buy a shovel or caviar. It is a very successful business. He told me about an employee who works harder than all other employees but doesn't do what they want done. "Does this person know what you want done?", I asked. "Yes", he replied, "but she still doesn't do it."

"Does the employee know how to do it?" I asked. "I don't know" was the reply. That, then, is the first issue to address. Once that is done, and assuming performance doesn't change, do they need this person? The answer is obvious. But they will have done all that can be done.

Chapter 5
Selling Is a Numbers Game

Direct mail is one means of selling products and services in a wide variety of markets. Companies who sell by direct mail know that a certain percentage of their mailings will result in orders being placed. There are several other things they know:

1. The average order value resulting from a particular direct mailing campaign (from historical data).
2. How much revenue they will need from each campaign to cover costs and ensure a profit.
3. Who the target market is.

Broadway Publications sells, among other things, A-Year-At-A-Time appointment books in both a pocket-size and desk-size version. Their most successful market is small business owners. They buy a list of those individuals from one of several sources.

The pocket-size version sells for $15 and the desk-size for $24. They know that, historically, a direct mail campaign to sell these appointment books will yield a 5 percent return on the pocket-size book and 3 percent return on the desk-size book. Therefore, a million mailings will bring in 50,000 orders at $15 for a total of $750,000. and 30,000 orders at $24 for a total of $720,000. Total revenues are $1,470,000.

Their pre-tax profit goal is 12 percent so they have kept printing, mailing and administrative costs, along with cost of goods at a level that will guarantee that pre-tax profit goal.

Their sales funnel is simple and straightforward. (See Figure 5.1.) No qualifying, presentations (except for the mailing piece itself), demonstrations, surveys, follow-up, and closing/negotiating steps are needed.

But the sales funnel doesn't reflect which of these steps are essential to ensuring they meet their sales and profit goals. It also

Figure 5.1
The Broadway Publications Sales Funnel

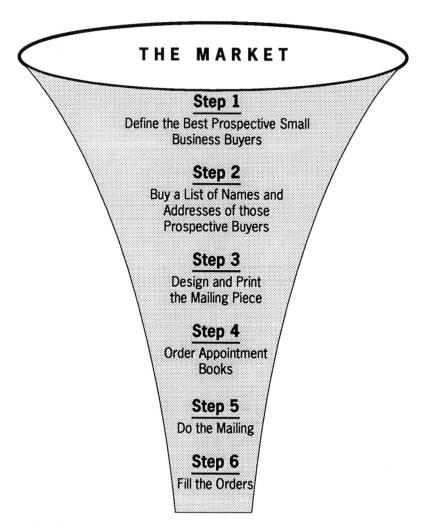

THE MARKET

Step 1
Define the Best Prospective Small
Business Buyers

Step 2
Buy a List of Names and
Addresses of those
Prospective Buyers

Step 3
Design and Print
the Mailing Piece

Step 4
Order Appointment
Books

Step 5
Do the Mailing

Step 6
Fill the Orders

doesn't reflect how many of each of the essential steps is needed to reach those goals.

Broadway Publications knows that they must buy 1,000,000 names at Step 2 so that becomes an essential step. Those names will generate the revenue and profit they want when they have finished Step 6 for this particular campaign. All six steps are obviously important. If they inaccurately define "the best prospective small business buyers" or the mailing piece is poorly designed, sales would be negatively impacted although it is difficult to estimate by how much. But if those two steps were performed to Broadway Publication's standards and they only bought 500,000 names, sales and profit goals will be reduced by 50 percent.

Establishing activity levels at your essential steps is critical to predicting your sales results as well. Establishing activity levels for certain sales funnel steps helps you take control of several critical sales management issues:

1. Knowing in advance if sales goals will be met or not
2. Accurately (and objectively) identifying performance weaknesses
3. Determining what training or development programs are needed to address those weaknesses
4. Determining how many salespeople are needed to meet company sales goals
5. Improving sales forecast accuracy
6. Determining appropriate courses of action to correct substandard performance
7. Setting sales and activity objectives with representatives (also known as agents) and dealers (also known as distributors) when you may be concerned about their willingness to take direction since they are "independent" business people

If you are having difficulty with one or more of these issues, this chapter will show you how to resolve each of them using the steps of the sales funnel as the basis for resolving them.

Previous chapters have emphasized that managing sales performance means managing activity at each step of the sales funnel. These are the performance standards for each step that were discussed in detail in Chapter 3.

What Are Sales Activity Levels?

American Chemical, for example, expects one order (sale) per month. They know that it takes the following levels of activity to get that order on the average:

1. Four pre-qualifying contacts to get one face-to-face sales meeting
2. Two face-to-face sales meetings to get one qualified prospect
3. Two qualified prospects to get two research tests and two presentations
4. Two sales presentations to get one production test

5.   Two production tests to get one order (sale)

Therefore, to get one new order (sale), an American Chemical salesperson should have:

- 64 Pre-qualifying contacts
- 16 Face-to-face contacts
- Eight qualified prospects
- Four research tests and presentations
- Two production tests

Measuring these activity levels allows American Chemical's sales managers to monitor performance without having to be with each salesperson on each call. If a sales manager sees that a salesperson has made only 34 pre-qualifying contacts and four face-to-face contacts in a given month, it is most likely that the salesperson will not get one new order. The activity in those two steps must be increased to the standards.

There are a few American Chemical salespeople who meet the one new order per month goal without meeting all the activity goals. They represent about 10 to 20 percent of the American Chemical sales force. Based on my experience, this percentage holds true in all sales organizations. This means, of course, that 80 to 90 percent need to be kept focused on the activity goals constantly and consistently. The majority of American Chemical Company's salespeople must reach required activity levels to reach the sales goal.

It isn't necessary to insist that those in the top 10 percent of your sales organization meet the activity goals unless they fall below the sales goal once. I have had many salespeople ask me this question, "Why do I have to make the required number of sales calls when Jack doesn't make them?" My answer is this, "When you are exceeding your sales quota, you don't have to make them either."

However, meeting the activity goals will predictably lead to meeting sales goals. You will recall one of my clients, Acme Northeast in Boston, who sells papers, films and chemicals to graphic arts shops around the country. Acme Northeast are in an extremely competitive marketplace where price becomes a major factor since these graphic arts papers, films and chemicals products are most often considered to be commodity items by end users. In order for Acme to grow, each salesperson must do what is expected from management.

They sell entirely by phone and each salesperson is required to make 70 outgoing business phone calls daily—Acme Northeast knows from historical data that it takes 70 outgoing business calls daily to reach and exceed sales goals. This may seem like a great many calls to some of you but a newly hired Acme salesperson who came from AT&T was accustomed to making 100 outgoing phone calls. Their assumption is that roughly 20 to 30 percent will be personal calls and they want to end up with 70 outgoing business phone calls daily. Each salesperson is required to enter the following information on the form shown in Figure 5.2 daily:

1. Outgoing number of business phone calls and accumulated variance
2. Number of orders and accumulated variance
3. Sales dollars sold and accumulated variance
4. Gross margin dollars and accumulated variance (gross margin is most important because their salespeople are paid incentive compensation based on gross margin, not sales—incentive compensation is discussed just before this chapter's summary)

The reason Acme Northeast uses accumulated variances is to keep their salespeople focused on daily goals and what must be done to catch up if they are below the goal at any given point in time.

This form is also used to develop weekly accumulated summaries by district. Figure 5.3 shows an accumulated summary through three weeks. Each line reflects accumulated totals for each salesperson in that district for those three weeks.

Acme Northeast's management knows that sales goals would have been met if the call levels had been met. As you look at Figure 5.3, you will see that some salespeople wouldn't have reached the sales goal by simply meeting call goals. But in several instances they discovered that the salespeople were making many personal calls.

Figure 5.3 reveals other things that help management pinpoint performance weaknesses:

1. Calls per order—Phil and Mary have higher than average calls per order. This indicates one or more of several possibilities:
   a) The salespeople did not qualify effectively.
   b) The presentation was ineffective.
   c) The salespeople did not ask for the order, or gave up too easily.
   Whatever the case, Acme Northeast management can listen on calls to determine just what the problem is.
2. Bob and Sam's calls were well below standard. They would have come much closer to their goals as indicated by the last line in Figure 5.3 —"Sales + if Call Goal Met"— that indicates how much more they would have sold if the sales call goal had been met. It is calculated based on actual dollars per call multiplied by the number of calls below the goal.

Figure 5.2
Daily Progression Form

Daily Progression Goal—Monday, October 12 to Friday, Oct 23

Daily Gross Margin: 947   Salesperson _____

Weeks 3 and 4	Mon Oct 12	Tue Oct 13	Wed Oct 14	Thu Oct 15	Fri Oct 16	Mon Oct 19	Tue Oct 20	Wed Oct 21	Thu Oct 22	Fri Oct 23	Totals
70 Calls											
Difference											
Minimum Orders	10	10	10	10	10	10	10	10	10	10	100
Actual											
Accum. Difference											
Sales Goal	2,871	2,871	2,871	2,871	2,871	2,871	2,871	2,871	2,871	2,871	28,710
Actual											
Accum. Difference											
Gross Margin Goal	947	947	947	947	947	947	947	947	947	947	9,470
Actual											
Accum. Difference											

3.   Tom exceeded his goal but didn't reach the sales call goal. Tom is a newly hired experienced graphic arts telephone salesperson and it is possible that his goal was too low.

Examples of other kinds of forms used to monitor performance and what should be done specifically to remedy the performance weaknesses shown in Figure 5.3 will be discussed in detail in Chapters 6 and 7. My purpose here is simply to show how important a diagnostic tool Figure 5.3 is if used properly and monitored weekly.

Goal-Setting Principles

There are several important issues to consider when setting any goal or series of goals:

1.   Goals must be established mutually between the salesperson and management whenever possible so that the salesperson has "ownership" of the goals.
2.   The goal must be achievable. There is nothing more frustrating than being given or agreeing to a goal that cannot realistically be met.
3.   The goal must not be too easy to reach and exceed. In the first place, if everyone meets or goes right past the goals too easily, there is no challenge. In the second place, upping the goals to be more challenging creates frustration for the salespeople because the goals now appear to be too hard and they don't think they can meet them.

Why did American Chemical choose the following steps to measure:

1.   Pre-qualifying
2.   Face-to-face sales meetings
3.   Qualified prospects
4.   Sales presentations
5.   Production tests

American Chemical salespeople must manage a great many activities each month. They don't have the time or resources to waste on unqualified prospects. It reinforces the need to do an effective job of pre-qualifying and qualifying prospects.

On the surface, it would seem that if a prospect was qualified, the rest of the steps would occur like clockwork and an order would be

Figure 5.3
Accumulative Summary

Sales District 1—Accumulative Summary—Week Ending October 16

Week 3	Bob	Sam	Phyllis	Brian	Phil	Mary	Tom	Totals
980 Calls	869	678	985	936	1,124	963	819	6,374
Difference	-111	-302	+5	-44	+144	-17	-161	-484
Minimum Orders	140	140	140	140	56	28	42	686
Actual	98	59	74	96	50	42	47	466
Difference	-42	-81	-66	-44	-6	+14	+5	-220
Sales Goal	40,194	40,194	40,194	40,194	15,264	8,484	11,158	196,042
Actual	33,810	18,636	28,287	30,483	15,340	9,039	13,656	149,251
Difference	-6,384	-21,558	-11,907	-9,711	-284	+555	+2,498	-46,791
Gross Margin Goal	13,258	13,258	13,258	13,258	5,152	2,800	3,682	64,666
Actual	10,157	6,148	9,096	10,714	4,827	3,027	4,930	48,899
Difference	-3,101	-7,110	-4,162	-2,544	-325	+227	+1,248	-15,767
Calls per Order	9	11	13	10	22	23	17	14
Dollars per Order	345	316	382	318	307	215	291	320
Sales + If Call Goal Met	5,306	9,142	116	7,182	0	401	2,810	24,958

assured. However, every step in their sales process doesn't go like clockwork. No sales process goes like clockwork.

American Chemical uses these steps to measure the kinds of things that might have gone wrong at any particular step. Several examples follow:

Example 1. If a salesperson makes 64 pre-qualifying sales contacts and gets only five face-to-face meetings, several things could be wrong: a) The wrong types of prospects were called; b) The decision maker or influencer wasn't reached; c) The salesperson didn't ask the right pre-qualifying questions.

This particular situation is a problem at Acme Northeast as well. Their telephone salespeople have a written list of qualifying questions they must ask on every initial prospect phone contact. This list is posted at each salesperson's workstation. When they don't ask these questions, and are asked to explain why, the response typically is, "Oh, I forgot," or it seemed "inappropriate at the time." When the sales situation is reviewed, it invariably turns out that it was, in fact, the appropriate time and the questions clearly should have been asked. They agree to do it and do it for a while. Then they fall back into old habits and "forget" or give some invalid reason for not asking them. They are then refocused and get back to the questions once again.

The point here is that simply giving a salesperson pre-qualifying and qualifying questions does not mean they are used consistently. You may assume the questions you have developed are used consistently but the only way to tell if that is so is to make joint sales calls or measure the ratios.

Example 2. If American Chemicals 16 face-to-face calls result in only three qualified prospects, several things could be wrong:

a) They weren't properly pre-qualified. Appointments were made with unqualified prospects—perhaps even forced on a prospect. This happens quite often at American Chemical. The salespeople know they need 16 face-to-face calls each month and will push for them (whether pre-qualified or not) to meet the activity goal and please management.

 That is why it is so important to measure the ratio. American Chemical expects the face-to-face calls to be pre-qualified according to the standard. If they are not, the salespeople aren't fooling management—they are only fooling themselves. And they will be caught at it every time.

 It is important to reemphasize that American Chemical doesn't use these measurements to catch their salespeople lying. It is to ensure they are performing to standard—doing the right things on every call as expected and as agreed to. It is the ongoing management process of making sure that their salespeople are doing what they are supposed to do.

b) The qualifying step was performed improperly. The right questions weren't asked on the face-to-face contact. Again, these ratios can lead the manager to question whether this step was performed to standard—to ensure the salespeople are doing what is expected.

c) The salesperson isn't talking to the right person. Many times, an initial prospect contact will say he/she makes the decision but on the face-to-face call, it turns out that isn't true. At that point, it is difficult to get to the right person without embarrassing the initial contact by going over his or her head. So the face-to-face call can become a waste of time.

American Chemical's sales managers can determine which of these three is the problem by making several face-to-face calls with their salespeople. It is most important with the newer salespeople. You might think that asking the salespeople to review the qualifying questions they asked would suffice but it does not. They may believe they asked the right questions when they really did not. It is not that they are lying—they just believed they asked those questions.

I have made hundreds of joint sales calls with salespeople who missed one or more important qualifying questions and when I asked why they missed them, the response was typically one of the following:

"I did ask that when I said…" or

"I know I missed it—I don't know why but I'll call him back and ask that question."

I would never have known they were missed if I hadn't made those calls. At Acme Northeast, phone calls are monitored according to the rules and regulations covering monitoring customer phone calls for training purposes. It is the only way to know what really happens on a sales call. You must make joint calls or listen in on calls if you have telemarketers or telephone salespeople to hear what salespeople say.

One important point about monitoring telephone conversations for training purposes—there are FCC and state regulations regarding monitoring phone conversations. Check with your attorney to find out what they are but remember to emphasize that you are monitoring them for training purposes only. In most cases it is legal as long as each salesperson knows that sales calls will be monitored.

Example 3. If 8 qualified prospects result in only two research tests and sales presentations, several things could be wrong. Two are more common. The *first*, the prospect may not have seen the value of conducting a research test because the right business benefit statements based on prospect concerns and the basis for the buying decision weren't presented or weren't presented effectively.

This could happen if the salesperson didn't uncover prospect concerns and the basis for the buying decision—a problem at the qualifying step. It could also happen if the salesperson did uncover them at the qualifying step but didn't address them during the presentation. Once again, joint sales calls will determine just what the problem is.

The *second*, the prospect might have agreed to a research test but did not commit to doing business if the tests were successful. The salesperson might have said something like, "Why don't you test it to see if it meets spec and we'll see what happens"—activity for activity's sake, when the important question is, "If the test is successful, is there any reason why you wouldn't do business with American Chemical?"

A commitment for the research test only is not good enough. If the prospect has not committed to doing business with American Chemical if the tests are successful, why do them until that commitment has been made? It's a waste of time.

The main point here is that prospect commitments or agreements to any step in the sales funnel are only of value if the commitment to do business with your company has been made as well. Conversely, if eight qualified prospects resulted in eight research tests and eight presentations, it is probably because the salesperson is a great qualifier, performing all aspects of the qualifying step perfectly. The best salespeople are hard nosed qualifiers.

Example 4. If research tests and presentations to production test ratios are too high (more than 2:1), American Chemicals sales managers will look to see: a) Was there a commitment to do the Production Testing? or b) Was the Presentation performed to standard and were all rules followed? If their salespeople say that both of the above were done, the sales manager will make joint sales presentation calls to determine why the ratios are too high. He will focus on this step because the normal ratios are out of line.

Summary

Establishing, measuring and managing activity ratios is a critical piece of managing sales performance. As you can see, it helps American Chemical's sales managers identify just where a problem exists and what must be done to correct it.

One sales manager complained to me about a salesperson who couldn't close the sale. I asked him if that salesperson could ask the customer for the order and he said "yes." When I asked what the real problem was, he said that in most cases the prospect would say "no" when asked if he would place the order today. The problem then, I pointed out, is not at the closing step. The problem exists earlier in the sales funnel, and he needs to determine at which step. Without measuring activity ratios and then making joint sales calls, he will never determine the real problem.

Establishing Your Activity Ratios

Your activity ratios will result from determining which of your funnel steps are critical measurements of progress toward a sale and how many of each step are needed to reach the next step, and so on, until the sale is made.

If you don't have any activity ratio history, pick some numbers you feel are close, gain agreement with your salespeople and test them for two to three months. They may not be quite right at first and will need to be adjusted. You may also find that other steps should be included in the measurement and some you started with should not. But, in all probability, you have a good idea as to what steps are important and what activity numbers are reasonable.

List the steps you will use (from Chapters 3 and 4) to measure activity ratios and progress toward one order:

step# 1 _____   step name _____
step# 2 _____   step name _____
step# 3 _____   step name _____
step# 4 _____   step name _____
step# 5 _____   step name _____
step# 6 _____   step name _____
step# 7 _____   step name _____
step# 8 _____   step name _____

You must determine how many of each step are needed to reach the next step, and so on through the Closing step. This should be done from the last step up to the first step. It's much easier to start with the last step and build up to the beginning of the sales funnel. closing step #.

step # _____   number needed _____
step # _____   number needed _____
step # _____   number needed _____
step # _____   number needed _____
step # _____   number needed _____

step # _____   number needed _____
step # _____   number needed _____
step #1 _____   number needed _____

Activity Ratios and Management Issues

Critical management issues are listed below along with how you can resolve them using your activity ratios:

Advance Knowledge of Sales Performance

American Chemical has established new business quotas at $360,000. per year for each salesperson. They pay their salespeople a salary, and commission dollars on new business only. Their salaries cover a variety of activities, including account management to ensure their existing business is protected.

Note: A discussion about incentive compensation can be found just before this chapter's summary.

Each American Chemical new business sales order averages $30,000. Therefore, each salesperson is expected to add one new customer per month to reach the $360,000. annual goal. If any one salesperson doesn't have eight newly qualified prospects in the sales funnel each month, the chances are that quota won't be met. Their selling cycle (the time it takes from the initial new prospect contact to a sales order) is 90 days. The eight newly qualified prospects should result in one sales order in three months. That must be taken into account when planning annual revenues. For example, a new salesperson who began on January 1st won't get the first $30,000. sale until sometime in April or early May.

There is an expression commonly used in sales called "keeping the pipeline full." The "pipeline" is each step of the sales funnel. Suppose you wanted to can ten jars of pickles and store them but ran out of pickles before the seventh jar was filled. Your pipeline went dry. You don't want your salespeople's pipeline to go dry. They must keep the sales funnel full by meeting sales activity goals monthly. It is the only way to predict that sales goals will be met.

Accurately Identifying Performance Weaknesses

This was discussed earlier in the chapter with both Acme Northeast and the kinds of things that could go wrong when the activity ratios were out of kilter at American Chemical. Since they help you accurately and objectively identify what went wrong and at what step(s) it went wrong, you can take the appropriate action(s) to correct the problem(s).

Determining Needed Training

If one of your salespeople isn't performing to standard, and you have identified just what the problem is, your first action should be to provide further training. It will most likely be in one of four areas:

a) Product training (including the competition)
b) Applications training
c) Selling skills training
d) Major accounts selling strategies

A detailed description of these topics and how training should be developed and delivered can be found in Chapter 7.

Determining Size of Sales Force

You should ensure proper sales coverage to meet your sales goals. You have a certain geographic area from which your sales revenue will come. You want to be sure you don't have too few or too many salespeople trying to reach your revenue goals.

American Chemical wants to increase its new business sales by $7,200,000. this fiscal year. Since each salesperson's annual new business quota is $360,000, they need 20 salespeople to reach the goal. They currently have 17 salespeople so they need three more. The three new salespeople won't sell their first order until April because of the 90-day sales cycle so American Chemical must choose one of several options:

a) Hire and start the three new salespeople in their territories in October preceding the fiscal year.
b) Hire and start the three new salespeople in January and increase the quota for each existing salesperson to compensate for the loss of $90,000.00 in sales in January, $90,000.00 in sales in February, and $90,000.00 in sales in March.
c) Hire and start the three new salespeople in January and reduce the annual company goal by $270,000.00.

These decisions are typically made based on budget limitations: Can they afford to add three new salespeople in October prior to the start of the fiscal year? Is increasing existing salespeople's quotas realistic and achievable? Can they reduce the sales goal by $370,000 without negatively impacting other programs and/or jobs?

How many salespeople do you need to meet your sales goals?

Improving Sales Forecast Accuracy

American Chemical uses very specific guidelines to forecast sales and you should do the same. These guidelines are based on the probability that they will get the order (sale). The guidelines are based on 90, 60 and 30 percent probabilities.

Probability of 90 percent. The salesperson has completed all funnel steps and is waiting for the paperwork to be completed by the new customer. American Chemical only puts 90 percent probability accounts on their 30 day forecasts.

Probability of 60 percent. The salesperson has completed funnel steps to and including the research test and presentation. The production testing, proposal preparation and presentation and closing steps remain. A salesperson who has completed only these steps must give the account a 60 percent probability because of the problems that could occur. These problems were discussed in detail in Chapter 3.

Probability of 30 percent. The salesperson has completed the qualifying step only—all other steps remain. Remember, each probability represents the chances of getting the order (sale) in its entirety, not that percentage of the expected order value.

American Chemical's sales managers discuss with each salesperson what it will take to move accounts from 30 percent probability to 60 percent probability, and 60 percent probability to 90 percent probability. If these accounts don't move to the next probability level when they should, something has gone wrong, and the sales manager holds strategy discussions with his salespeople to find out what it is.

Account strategizing is an important sales management function. Many things can go wrong during the selling process. It is your responsibility to strategize with your salespeople about what it will take to move the sale from one step to the next logical step. It is not always necessary to go to the next step in the funnel sequence but rather the next logical step. For example, research testing may not be necessary if a decision person has worked with American Chemical in the past. They may be able to go right to the presentation and production testing steps.

Another situation that occurs all too frequently is the emergence of another decision person after a step toward the end of the funnel (e.g., production testing). It may be necessary for the salesperson to go back to the qualifying step with this new decision person to ensure that his concerns and reasons for making the buying decision are determined and addressed.

Too often, salespeople run into a dilemma with an account and don't discuss it with anyone else. It would be helpful if they were to call fellow salespeople and discuss the situation. Other salespeople often provide solutions that can get the sale moving in the right direction once again. But it is most helpful if your salespeople discuss these situations with you so you are aware of the problems that exist and can use your expertise to help rectify them.

Account strategizing becomes more focused because of the sales funnel steps. Since it can be identified at which step the sale seems to be stalled, strategizing will center on that step.

Correcting Substandard Performance

One of your primary roles is to help your salespeople be successful. This topic will be discussed in detail in Chapter 6 but it is appropriate to comment on it here. If a salesperson isn't doing what should be done, it is for one or more of the following reasons:

a) He or she doesn't know what is supposed to be done. For example, one sales manager said to me that he used to think that because he hired experienced salespeople, they should know how to manage a territory. But he found that most could not, and it taught him not to assume that salespeople know what to do, or what is to be done, simply because they have "experience."

b) He or she doesn't know how to do it. This sales manager found that even if his salespeople knew the importance of effective and efficient territory management, it didn't mean they knew how to manage the territory effectively.

c) Not being directed or managed to do it. If a sales manager isn't measuring territory management effectiveness and efficiency, it will become slipshod with 80 to 90 percent of the sales organization.

d) Not able to do it even if he or she knows what to do and how to do it. Some salespeople simply can't do the job and all the training in the world won't help. One sales manager told me that his company hired too many poor salespeople, trained them and wound up with trained poor salespeople.

e) Not caring one way or the other. Some salespeople don't care whether they are successful—they just want to draw a salary.

The first three (a, b and c) are training issues. The sales funnel will help identify what training is needed. Once your funnel is developed, your salespeople can be trained to do what they are expected to do and how to do it. And you can measure and manage performance.

The last two present a different set of problems. Further training might help but in all probability termination will be the result. It's always difficult to terminate an employee, but in far too many cases sales managers allow substandard performers to slide, and slide, and slide even more without taking the right corrective action. A consistent substandard performer negatively affects the rest of the sales organization that questions why management lets it go on for so long. One sales manager told me that he was amazed at how many of his good salespeople thought that a substandard performer should have been terminated long before he decided to do it. This happens all too often.

In addition to negatively affecting the other members of the sales organization, you will be interested to see how a substandard performer negatively affects revenues. It is far greater than you might think as Figure 5.4 shows when two American Chemical salespeople perform at 50 percent of new business quota from January to June.

The two salespeople are terminated in June. There is $15,000 in sales from both their territories in July. Two new salespeople are hired and start in August. Since it takes 90 days for a new salesperson to get the first order, there are no sales in August, September and October. Assuming the two new salespeople do what is expected, sales will be $60,000 in November and December.

Two substandard performers have caused a $405,000 shortfall for the year because the sales manager waited far too long to take action. Dealing with this type of problem will be discussed in detail in Chapter 6.

Figure 5.4
Substandard Performance Is Shown from January Through June

Month	Sales	Sales Shortfall
January	30,000	30,000
February	30,000	60,000
March	30,000	90,000
April	30,000	120,000
May	30,000	150,000
June	30,000	180,000
July	15,000	225,000
August	0	285,000
September	0	345,000
October	0	405,000
November	60,000	405,000
December	60,000	405,000

As difficult as you might find this to believe, I have had many sales managers tell me that a substandard performer is at least a known quantity—that the poor performance can at least be counted on—and replacing that person with someone new might result in even poorer performance. Is it conceivable that the new person might perform at quota? Of course!

Setting Sales Objectives with Representatives

What are representatives (or agents)? They are either individuals or small companies with a few salespeople who represent a number of companies who don't want to or can't afford to hire salespeople to penetrate their defined marketplace. Representatives typically know many of the decision people in accounts you want to penetrate in certain geographic areas. They are paid a commission for selling your products and/or services but you do the billing, maintain and ship inventory and are responsible for customer support and service. This allows you to control pricing, support and service. In many companies, it is desirable to maintain as much control at the customer level as is possible.

What are dealers (or distributors)? They typically are companies, both large and small, with several sales, service and support personnel. They differ from representatives in that they buy products from you at a discounted price and sell them at prices the dealers determine, regardless of your suggested pricing and are responsible for service and support. The end user becomes the dealer's customer, not yours. Control over pricing, service and support (and therefore your company's reputation) depend on the strength and integrity of the dealer.

Copier and facsimile manufacturers typically use dealers. Even IBM uses computer dealers to sell their home and office computer products and services. It is the least expensive alternative to reach that marketplace.

Why do so many companies believe that representatives and dealers can't be managed the way direct salespeople can? Because they really haven't tried. They assume they can't be managed, or won't accept management because they are independent business people.

I can tell you from experience that good representatives or dealers want to be successful with the products they handle and will accept all the help they can get. Many of them have told me the products that are most difficult to sell or get the least emphasis by their salespeople are those from manufacturers who don't provide support (training, brochures, joint sales calls, etc.). They want to be treated just as a direct salesperson would be treated—as a part of the companies they represent.

Many manufacturers feel that representatives and dealers are the experts in their fields, that's why they chose them and they can do it on their own. It doesn't work that way. If you think that representatives and dealers might be right for your company in specific geographic areas, you have to deal with them just as you would a direct salesperson. You should:

a) Interview several
b) Outline your goals and expectations for them and how they will be measured
c) Gain their agreement that the goals will be met
d) Clearly state what you will do to support them
e) Ask for and check references (accounts they now do business with)
f) Select one
g) Take appropriate actions if they don't meet performance goals (discussed in detail in Chapter 6)

Incentive Compensation

This book will not go into incentive compensation in great detail, but there are some issues you should consider when establishing a commission plan.

Studies show that many successful companies don't pay commissions at all. Digital Equipment Corporation is one. These companies are typically very well known and have outstanding products that are clearly the performance leaders in their industries. Many salespeople want to be associated with industry leaders—it makes selling easier, with less customer resistance.

These companies know that their customers need to be serviced by their salespeople on a consistent basis and believe that salespeople won't want to provide a high level of ongoing service if they are paid commissions for what they sell. They will want to spend time with accounts who are likely to buy a new product.

Servicing existing accounts will obviously bring additional business but calling on new accounts is necessary as well and that is where incentive compensation can help tremendously.

In my experience, the best salespeople expect to receive incentive compensation. That is what motivates many of them. Many others are happy to be rewarded by plaques for performance excellence or other such expressions of recognition (trips, dinners for two, etc.). Recognition is almost as important as the monetary rewards for many salespeople. They want to feel that the company recognizes outstanding performance and money alone doesn't provide that feeling. That is why many companies provide such things as:

1. "Salesperson of the month" plaques (you have seen employee of the month photographs in supermarkets and other retail outlets).
2. A parking space next to the President for the "salesperson of the month" for the next month
3. President's clubs (often called by other names) where salespeople who exceed certain performance standards for a given period of time go to a resort area for a week (with spouses or, if single, another person) with company executives and the other President's club members. They are wined and dined and made to feel very important. There is always an awards ceremony where they receive their plaques, rings or other President's club mementos from the President and have their pictures taken with the president.
    I know of salespeople who will do whatever it takes to become a President's club member without thinking about the incentive compensation that goes with it. Recognition for outstanding performance is what matters most (although they certainly don't volunteer to give the money back).
4. Monthly contests for specific areas of excellence with cash awards. For example, Acme Northeast gives each salesperson $200. in cash if they exceed a certain dollar volume for a particular product that provides a high gross margin.

Incentive compensation is especially effective when designed to support specific and challenging sales goals. American Chemical wants $30,000. in new business from each salesperson each month and customers aren't knocking their doors down to buy products. That is why they chose to provide incentive compensation on new business—to direct their salespeople toward the more difficult challenge. It is much easier and more comfortable for salespeople to go back to existing customers for new business. Cold calling is much harder on many salespeople's egos—they have difficulty with the rejection that is a natural part of cold calling.

In addition to bringing in new business, incentive compensation can help with a) upgrading customers to new products or new product enhancements, b) penetrating new markets where the company may not have much experience, c) selling service agreements on hardware products, and d) improving gross margins.

Most companies pay incentive compensation based on sales. They believe they can meet gross margin goals by controlling pricing. However, in highly competitive industries, price erosion is common. In addition, discounts come in other forms such as free shipping, 30-day money back guarantees, free service, free support, toll free 800 numbers to name but a few. They all tend to erode gross margin, which really is the bottom line—the most important number on which to focus.

For example, Acme Northeast sells in a highly competitive marketplace where the average gross margin on graphic arts papers, films and chemicals typically averages 12 to 17 percent. However, Acme's margins are close to 32 percent, largely because their salespeople are paid on the amount of gross margin resulting from each sale. It is clearly better for Acme Northeast to sell $50,000 worth of material at 32 percent gross margin than $100,000 at 12 percent. Not only do they make more profit but enjoy several other benefits: a) inventory levels are lower, b) receivables are lower, c) less support people are needed, and d) they don't pay commissions on sales dollars that provide a lower gross margin than they now achieve by paying commissions on gross margin.

One of my clients is changing their incentive compensation from sales to gross margin. They are also in a highly competitive and price sensitive marketplace. But they have added a wrinkle to the plan. They add a percentage onto the cost of the rugs that will lock in a specific profit amount they need and then let the salespeople sell the products for anywhere between that number and the suggested list price. The compensation plan pays almost no commission if the rug sells for the lowest price. Commission percentages then increase as the actual selling price gets closer to the suggested retail price. So the incentive is there for their salespeople to sell at list or as close to list as is possible.

Incentive compensation plans should be simple for your salespeople to understand. If they are complicated to calculate (as many are), your salespeople will have difficulty figuring out how much they will make at various sales levels or how much they need to sell to make what they want to make.

Total compensation (at 100 percent of quota) should not exceed what comparable salespeople in comparable industries earn in your geographical area. However, if your salespeople exceed quota, there should not be a limit on the amount of incentive compensation they can earn. Unfortunately, many companies "cap" (put a ceiling on) compensation, which defeats its purpose.

Consider the foregoing issues when developing an incentive compensation plan. Incentive compensation can help you achieve your sales and profit goals.

Chapter Summary

You have determined which of your sales funnel steps are critical indicators of progress toward a sale and you have determined what activity levels are necessary at each step.

You can now meet with your salespeople (or representatives and/or dealers) and put the steps in place. If you do, you will no longer be as concerned with those seven critical management issues.

Chapter 6
Expect, Inspect

Y ou have established your performance standards at each step of the sales funnel (Chapters 3 and 4) and the ratios necessary to measure sales performance (Chapter 5). You must have a formal way to measure the performance of your salespeople. If you "expect" certain levels of performance, you must have a way to "inspect" to be sure your expectations are met. The most common ways are by utilizing a variety of sales reports. This chapter discusses:

1. Whether you need to use reports at all
2. How to ensure you only ask your salespeople for reports that are meaningful and why that is so important
3. The kinds of reports you should use and how frequently you should get and use them
4. Examples of those reports (that you can redesign to meet your specific needs)
5. How to use them as performance measurement tools

These five issues will be discussed one at a time.

Why Have Reports?

Reports can be either verbal or written. Most of the discussions in this chapter deal with formal, written reports. However, it is necessary for you to determine what reports are needed in your organization and, if so, should they be written or verbal reports.

In very small sales organizations (one or two outside salespeople or two to three inside salespeople), written reports may not be necessary. You may talk to your salespeople daily and can verbally gather the necessary information to measure critical activity ratios during those conversations. You know just what is going on in each account being worked, whether they are properly qualified, what the next step in the sales process should be and when it should happen.

However, many sales managers tell me they don't have the time to talk to or meet with their salespeople on a regular basis because of other job priorities. Sales management is typically not the sole responsibility of most managers in small to medium-size organizations. Even in larger organizations, sales managers have said they can only spend 20 percent to 30 percent of their time with their salespeople in accoun- related activities.

While it is true that sales managers have other responsibilities (such as customer service, applications support, marketing activities, strategic planning, budget management, paperwork, a variety of meetings and "firefighting" to name but a few), it is also true that managing salespeople is the least-liked activity. Typically, it is due to not knowing what to manage so it is avoided and seems less important when compared to other responsibilities.

Meetings and Firefighting

It is worth taking a few minutes to discuss meetings and firefighting. There is no activity known to man that takes up more time than meetings. On how many occasions have you or your salespeople called someone only to find him or her in a meeting and unreachable? Many meetings are unnecessary, take too long and don't accomplish very much. The rule of thumb for meetings is to:

1. Prepare an agenda that includes the meeting objective (what is the desired meeting result) and circulate it to all participants several days prior to the meeting so they can prepare. Many people come to meetings unprepared, which wastes a lot of time.
2. Set a time frame for the meeting and stick to it.
3. Assign a meeting leader who must keep the meeting on the agenda items and not let it wander into unrelated areas.
4. The first agenda item should be to see if anyone has additional items to be added to the agenda. They can be discussed at that meeting or tabled for subsequent meetings.
5. If a specific, meaningful objective cannot be established, the meeting may be unnecessary.

"Firefighting" activities are an interesting phenomenon. Most sales managers tell me that even if they plan their day to the last minute, the plan goes out the window in the first 30 minutes because some unexpected emergency comes up. Firefighting activities are a part of every manager's daily routine and time for it should, therefore, be planned.

These two activities and other responsibilities clearly require your attention. But effectively managing your salespeople's activities is your most important activity, especially if they are not selling at standard. Other responsibilities should take second place to getting your salespeople performing to standard. As has been stated many times, that means monitoring critical funnel activities to ensure the desired sales results are likely to happen or to know in advance if they are not and take appropriate action.

Consequently, if you have other responsibilities that limit the time you have available for your salespeople, then you will need written reports if you are to keep up to speed on their activities. Otherwise, every phone or face-to-face meeting will require the salesperson to bring you up to speed on each account in the funnel because you are likely to forget. This is time consuming and frustrating for your salespeople. They prefer that you know what they are working on, what problems (if any) they are having, where the sale stands and what they are to do next so meaningful discussions can take place. If it isn't written down, you will have difficulty.

Meaningful Reports

Sales reports should provide the information you need to ensure your salespeople are doing the right things. You will see that sales reports are effective measurement and development tools regardless of the number of salespeople in your organization. They formalize the process you will use to discuss account strategies, detect performance weaknesses and develop your salespeople to improve sales performance.

You should use only reports that provide you with the information you need. You also should use only reports if you review them with your salespeople on a consistent basis. Salespeople don't like paperwork and sales reports are no exception. The major reason is that they see it as activity for activity's sake. This occurs when sales reports are misused by sales management—they aren't consistently reviewed with salespeople and, in many cases, are not reviewed at all. This is the major reason salespeople hate to fill out reports. They think reports are a way for sales management to "keep tabs" on them—they don't feel trusted. Sales reports must be reviewed consistently. They are designed to help your salespeople stay on track and stay focused—in short, they help your salespeople to be successful.

There is no sense in developing a report just because you think you should have one or someone told you that you should have one. For example, one sales manager told me he didn't think his salespeople were making enough sales calls so he arbitrarily established a goal of 20 calls per week. He didn't specify whether they should be calls on new accounts, could be repeat calls on the same account or any standards at all—just 20 calls each week. He also instituted a call report to ensure each salesperson made 20 calls.

One day he showed me a three-foot stack of call reports covering a three-month period. None had been reviewed with the salespeople. His complaint was that everyone made 20 calls as required but sales hadn't increased at all. Two issues were obvious: *First,* he got what he wanted—call reports with 20 calls listed. There was no way to tell if the calls were actually made—the reports were not reviewed with the salespeople. Actually, the calls were reported "to make him happy," "keep him off our backs."

Second, the goal was 20 calls per week. Nothing was said about increased sales. All the mistakes that could be made were made in this situation. It was activity for activity's sake and not directed toward increasing sales.

If you institute sales reports, make sure they tell you what you need to know and use them in regular phone or face-to-face meetings to keep your salespeople focused and assist in account strategizing to help get the order.

Meeting Checklist

The following should be discussed at performance review meetings: the itinerary, the call report, expense reports (if appropriate due to an identified problem), sales forecasts, lost order reports, and goals and plans for the next month.

There are several reports that are typically used:

1. Call report—a document that salespeople fill out and send to management, summarizing sales activity over a specified period of time.
2. Itinerary—a document that tells sales management on which accounts a salesperson plans to make sales calls over a specified period of time.
3. Sales forecasts—documents that tell sales management which accounts will close and when over a specified period of time.
4. Lost order reports—documents that detail the reasons why an order was lost, either to competition or because of a decision not to do anything now.

Each of these types of reports will be discussed in detail so you can determine which of them are appropriate for your organization. The major point to remember is that sales reports should be used to help keep your salespeople focused on the main target—appropriate sales activity that will lead to an order. That means they must be reviewed with your salespeople on a scheduled basis. One of the most difficult management tasks is finding the time necessary to review reports consistently. For some reason, sales managers don't like to do it. It can become confrontational and many sales managers don't like confrontations with their own people.

However, it is the most important sales development task that sales managers must perform. It provides a methodology for staying on top of just what salespeople are doing. You can't be with them most of the time so these vehicles help you to analyze what they are doing right, what they are doing wrong and what to do about it. Most salespeople like to review the status of each account so strategies can be developed. You can provide strategic support.

If a report isn't reviewed on a regular basis, don't use it. If it doesn't help salespeople improve performance, it's a waste of time.

The Itinerary and Call Reports

The itinerary and call reports will be discussed together for one primary reason—they can be completed on the same forms which saves salespeople excessive paperwork.

The Itinerary tells you what your salespeople plan to do. The call report tells you what they did. These are the most important reports. They form the basis for account strategizing, salesperson development, the foundation for measuring critical activity ratios and the ability to manage those ratios.

American Chemical Company requires their salespeople to fill out an itinerary and call report weekly. Some companies require it weekly or monthly but weekly is most common.

Figure 6.1 shows their itinerary and call report form. It is designed for outside salespeople (a telemarketing example will be shown later in this chapter).

This form can be 8 1/2" by 11". However, I have seen some larger, depending on the amount of information to be gathered. The size of the form doesn't matter; getting the right information does. The report shouldn't be over complicated. The specific information American Chemical requires includes:

1. Planned call date
2. Company name
3. Key contact and title—this is an important issue for their sales managers because it shows whether the salespeople are calling at the right levels, depending upon the call objective.

Figure 6.1
Weekly Itinerary/Call Report

American Chemical Company – Weekly Itinerary/Call Report

Salesperson _____

Date	Company Name	Key Contact/Title	Call Objective	Step	Call Result	Next Action

4. Call objective—they want to know specifically what the salesperson expects to accomplish that will move the sale to the next funnel step
5. Step (of the funnel)—their salespeople simply enter a letter designation for the appropriate funnel step. Their funnel steps with letter designations follow:

> Step 1—PA = Pre-approach call—initial phone contact
> Step 2—I = Initial follow-up sales call (face-to-face) (qualifying and gaining commitments)
> Step 3—T = Submit a product for testing
> Step 4—FT = Follow-up on the testing
> Step 5—S = Survey
> Step 6—SP = Sales presentation
> Step 7—TR = Trial production run
> Step 8—FR = Follow-up the trial production run
> Step 9—PP = Proposal presentation
> Step 10—PF = Proposal follow-up
> Step 11—C = Close (final objections and Negotiations as well)
> Step 12—AM = Provide account management

The steps form the basis for developing critical selling ratios.

6. Call result—What happened on the call? Was the objective met?
7. Next action—What specifically will happen next? It's essential to know what their salespeople plan to do next.

Report Format and How It Is Used

American Chemical's itinerary and call report are a three-part, multicolored, carbon form. Items one to five are filled in by their salespeople during the week prior to the planned calls. The salesperson keeps the white copy and sends the pink copy to the sales manager so he/she has it by Monday morning of the week the calls will be made. This becomes the itinerary.

At the end of each sales call, the salespeople are to write in the call result and next action. Many salespeople do it at the end of the day but it is clearly best to do it immediately after the sales call while call particulars are fresh in the salespeople's minds. The copy for the past week is sent along with the itinerary so the sales manager has both on Monday morning. This becomes the call report.

The sales manager now has last week's actual activities and next week's planned activities. The manager can discuss both with each salesperson. You will see why it is important to have both.

In order for American Chemical's sales managers to have the reports by Monday morning, they must be "faxed" over the weekend. Some of their sales managers require it by Friday afternoon so they can review the documents over the weekend. Others want to give the salesperson time to complete the Friday's activities and come into the office over the weekend or early Monday morning to review them. It makes little difference so long as there is sufficient time to review them.

The major point here is that if your salespeople must mail their reports rather than "fax" them, they will have to do it earlier in the week. I have had sales managers tell me that their salespeople couldn't get these two reports in by the weekend because they would have to mail them on Wednesday, two and one-half days before the end of the week. If that is the case, then simply make the weekly itinerary and call report cover Thursday through Wednesday. The time period doesn't matter. Gathering the information does.

American Chemical's call report and itinerary has 12 lines on which to record calls. Salespeople send in another copy if they plan more than 12 calls.

Follow-up and Review

American Chemical's sales managers talk with each salesperson on Monday morning and review the call report and itinerary in detail. They have allotted each salesperson 45 minutes on a scheduled basis (salesperson #1, 8:30–9:15, salesperson #2, 9:15–10:00, and so on). Each salesperson calls the sales manager at the beginning of the allotted time. The salesperson may be at home or on the road but is expected to call at the allotted time.

A completed itinerary (Figure 6.2), the call report for that week (Figure 6.3), a pre-approach call summary (Figure 6.4) and another itinerary (Figure 6.5) are shown along with the types of questions their sales managers ask the salespeople (along with my comments when appropriate). You should use these questions and comments as a guide to the types of questions you need to ask.

With the exception of a salesperson's first week, American Chemical's sales managers review the call report first. They want to know what happened during the last weekly period to ensure the right mix of call activity and issues that might affect planned activity for the subsequent weekly period.

For these four examples, however, we will start with the itinerary (Figure 6.2) even though this is an experienced salesperson. We have

Figure 6.2
Itinerary/Call Report—Example 1

American Chemical Company – Weekly Itinerary/Call Report

Salesperson _Bob Johnson_

Date	Company Name	Key Contact/Title	Call Objective	Step	Call Result	Next Action
Mon 5-27	Home pre-approach calls	—	Pre qualify for Appointments	PA		
Tues 5-28	Memphis Oil	Jim Carney Purchasing Mgr	determine proposal results	PF		
Tues 5-28	Barton Oil	Henry Orst Production Mgr	Sales presentation get authorization for initial run	SP		
Wed 5-29	Aqua Oil	Henry Gorc Purchasing	Determine his concerns about delivery - fix	AM		
Wed 5-29	Boyd Co.	Jim Hurley Research	get commitment for a research test	T		
Thur 5-30	watson Oil	Jim watson President	F.U. on pre-Approach call	I		
Thurs 5-30	smith oil	Barry McDonald Prod. Mgr	F.U. on pre-approach call	I		
Fri 6-31	Mission oil	Bob Jakes Purchasing	F.U. on Pre-approach call	I		
Fri 5-31	James Oil	will cahill Purchasing	Review contract details re: payment sched.	AM		

137

to start somewhere. Refer to the figures as you read the questions and comments that follow.

There are several types of questions the sales manager will raise for each day's planned activities (comments follow certain questions in parentheses—more detailed information appears under Comments)

Monday, May 27—a pre-approach call day

"How many calls do you plan to make today?"

"When will you give me a detailed summary of your phone calls?"

"Why haven't you planned a face-to-face sales call for the afternoon?"

Comment: American Chemical salespeople use Monday to make pre-approach phone calls—typically for one-half day. That is why the sales manager asked about a face-to-face sales call. There may be a good answer and there may not be. The sales manager simply wants to know "why" so he can make certain this salesperson is focused.

The sales manager must have a written summary of phone calls (see Figure 6.5). Otherwise, there is no way to monitor that activity. One sales manager showed me a call report that stated "made phone calls" for each day of an entire week. I asked why it wasn't important to know who had been called and what the results were. He said that the salesperson was an experienced professional and if he said he made the calls, he made the calls! This salesperson was terminated three months later for non-performance by the sales manager's immediate supervisor. Why the sales manager's boss? Because the sales manager still didn't know how to or chose not to measure sales activity, and the lack of performance on this salesperson's part didn't seem to matter to the sales manager one way or another. He simply assumed the business would come because this salesperson had many years of industry sales experience. It might not surprise you to learn that the sales manager was terminated some six months later for non-performance as well.

Tuesday, May 28

Memphis Oil—"How many people have reviewed the Proposal?"

"Will you see the other decision people on this visit?" (It's important to see them all, obviously. It would have been nice if the salesperson had planned to see them all this time around.)

Barton Oil Co.—"How many decision people will be at the presentation?"

"If you can't get them all there, when can you get to the other ones?"

"What supporting materials are you taking with you?"

Wednesday, May 29

Aqua Oil—"When did they start having delivery problems?" (The
sales manager might not have known about them before.)
"What type of problem are they having?" (late deliveries,
damaged shipments, etc.)
"How do you plan to make sure the problem gets corrected?"
"Will that satisfy Henry Gove?"
"What will you do if it doesn't?"

Boyd Oil Co.—"Jim Hurley has agreed to test our product, as I recall.
Is that right?"
"You'll confirm a date for the test, won't you?"
"If a date is confirmed, you'll follow up to make sure they test it
when they said they would?"
"Now that you've put this much time and effort into Boyd, what
will you do if Hurley doesn't agree to do the test, or puts it on
hold for some reason?" (wants to be sure the salesperson has a
strategy for these eventualities)

Thursday, May 30

Watson Co.—"How is it that you are able to see the President?"
"This must be a smaller company. Are they Qualified?" (The
sales manager doesn't expect much from this call if the
salesperson can see the president.)

Smith Oil—"Did they say they would consider us on the pre-
approach phone call? If not, why not" (We should have
determined it on the phone call.)
"If you didn't call Barry McDonald, how do you know he'll be
there today?"
"Is McDonald the right person to make this decision? Are there
others who need to be involved? Who are they?"
Comment: There may be perfectly good answers to these
questions or there may not be. The sales manager is making sure
that the right things were done. If the answers are not the right
ones, the sales manager makes suggestions as to what should be
done, up to and including not making the call at all if no pre-
approach information was gathered. It is difficult to see
important prospects without an appointment in American
Chemical's markets.

Friday, May 31

Mission Oil—(same questions and comments as was the case with
Smith Oil on Thursday)

James Oil—"How far behind in payments are they?"
"What does finance want them to agree to?" (better find out
before the call if the salesperson doesn't know)

Figure 6.3
Weekly Itinerary/Call Report—Example 2

American Chemical Company – Weekly Itinerary/Call Report
Salesperson _Bob Johnson_

Date	Company Name	Key Contact/Title	Call Objective	Step	Call Result	Next Action
Mon 5-27	Home Pre-approach calls		Pre-qualify for appointments	PA	Called 12 reached 10	Visit 2 new accounts/most timeous
Tues 5-28	Memphis Oil	Jim Carney Purchasing Mgr	Determine proposal results	PF	Jim couldn't see me	made appt for 5-12 prop. results
Tues 5-28	Barton Oil	Henry Best Production Mgr	Sales presentation set confirm. for trial run	SP	very impressed with our cap's	Prod. test run set for 6-17
Wed 5-29	Aqua Oil	Henry Gore Purchasing	Determine his concern w/ problem	AM	I said wld deliv. on sched	Meet with our sched. dept assure on time del.
Wed 5-29	Boyd Co.	Jim Hurley Research	Get commitment for a research tst	T	agreed to a test	submit prod. & test 6-12
Thurs 5-30	Watson Oil	Jim Watson President	F.U. on pre-approach call	I	not enough volume	None
Thurs 5-30	Smith Oil	Barry McDonald Production Mgr	F.U. on pre-approach call	I	Qualified - wants research	Meet with research/site arg. test
Fri 5-31	Mission Oil	Bob Jakes Purchasing	F.U. on pre-approach call	I	happy with present supplier	Call again in 6 mos
Fri 5-31	James Oil	Will Cahill Purchasing	review contract details re: payment sched	AM	agreed to pay w/i 10 days	See if that is acceptable w/ finance

"What will finance do if they don't agree?" (wants to be sure they won't be put on COD or reduced shipments if they don't agree—will call finance to look for alternative solutions and discuss it with the salesperson before the sales call is made)

It is now Monday, June 3rd and the sales manager has received the call report from the previous week (Figure 6.3), the pre-approach call summary (Figure 6.4) and the itinerary (Figure 6.5) for this week. He will review the call report first.

Monday, May 27

The sales manager reviews the pre-approach phone call summary that was included with the call report and Itinerary (see Figure 6.4)

This report is very straightforward. American Chemical wants to be certain that calls are made on the right decision people and that they were pre-qualified. You will notice that there are hash marks in the final column (Annual $ Potential). The reason is quite simple. They want to know the potential of these accounts. Let's start with where appointments have not been made (left of the hash mark)—if there is enough potential but the salesperson was unable to get any commitments and an appointment, they will strategize about other ways to penetrate the account. The final column shows also where firm appointments have been made (right of the hash mark)—these are real possibilities, or should be.

In the summary at the bottom of the report, American Chemical wants to know the number of contacts—people actually reached, the number of firm appointments set, and the annual dollar potential for accounts where firm appointments have been set—"I's"

It isn't necessary to list the kinds of questions to be asked about this report—it's only necessary to discuss some interesting things it shows:

First, ABC Oil (the first call)—it appears that Jack Smith was in fact not pre-qualified—the salesperson should know whether ABC Oil will "consider" American Chemical as a supplier on the pre-approach call.

Second, six of the twelve calls were made on purchasing people. Two were not available—obviously this happens frequently on pre-approach calls in all businesses. Four expressed "no interest," "happy with our present supplier". The only interest generated was with decision people other than purchasing.

There is an important message here. It is difficult to sell purchasing people unless there is a real or perceived problem with the present supplier. They don't really care about the value issues American Chemical can offer. Production does. This doesn't mean that purchasing is never interested in value issues—it simply means that they typically are not.

Figure 6.4
Pre-Approach Call Summary

Pre-Approach Call Summary

Salesperson _Bob Johnson_ Date _5/27_

Company Name	Key Contact/Title	Comments	Next Step	Annual Potential
ABC Oil Co.	Jack Smith Prod. Mgr	Wants to see what our product can do	Face-to-face call to see if he'll consider	50K
Margin Co.	Andy King Purchasing	not available call again	—	
Bulk Oil	Bob Douglas Purchasing	no interest - happy w/ present supplier	call again in 6 months	65K
Gateway Oil	Mitchell Paul Prod'n Mgr	no interest - happy w/ present supplier	call again in 6 months	45K
Melville Oil	Barry waters Purchasing	no interest now but call again in July	F.U. phone call 7-8	35K
Brithy Oil	John Peters Purchasing	not available - will call again		
Wilson Oil	Jim Perkins Prod. Mgr	no interest - happy with present supplier	call again in 6 months	
Watery Oil	Paul Gibbons Production mgr	will see me in 3 months	call for appoint. 8-15	50K
Mills Co.	Ralph Cleary Research Dir	Told me to call Phil Brady Prod. mgr. not in	Call Brady 6-10	
Harris Oil	Jack Ink Purchasing	no interest - happy with present supp.	call again in 6 months	
Peanut Oil	Jim Higgins Prod Mgr	wants to see me in one month	call for an appt 6-20	25K

Contacts Made: _10_ Number of Appointments Set _1_ Annual $ Potential - "1s" _50K_

Third and finally, it would seem that the most important contacts are production people—that they are the best initial contacts. The sales manager will point these issues out to the salesperson and get his agreement to focus on production managers. He will also stress the importance of pre-qualifying.

The Balance of the Call Report

The sales manager continues through the call report: The sales manager's questions are followed by commentary in parenthesis and more detailed infomation under Comment.

Tuesday, May 28

Memphis Oil—"Why couldn't Jim see you?" (He was called to another meeting.)

"Couldn't he have let you know about it in advance?" (Jim just learned of the meeting that morning.)

"Were you able to find out if all decision people had reviewed the proposal?"

"Did you try to see one of them to get a reaction to the proposal? If not, why not?"

Comment: There is nothing the salesperson could have done about Jim's meeting. However, there have been situations where the appointment wasn't firm, or even agreed to up front. Once again, there may be perfectly good answers to the last two questions or there may not. The sales manager is attempting to keep the salesperson focused on the objective which was to get Proposal reaction, regardless of the contact.

Barton Oil—"It sounds like the presentation went extremely well. How many of the decision people were there?"

"Did all participants buy into the production test?" (In this case all did but in other situations some don't and it is important to find out who did or did not and what their concerns are. (asked if all didn't buy in)

"How do you think that will affect our ability to get their business?" "What do you think we should do about it?" (The sales manager is strategizing with the salesperson and coaching at the same time.)

Wednesday, May 29

Aqua Oil—"Was that solution satisfactory to Henry?" (It was, but the sales manager wanted to be sure.)

"Was the problem one of scheduling or was production late getting the product made?"

"Have you talked to our scheduling department yet?"

"When are they due for the next shipment? You'd best get to them well before that date, wouldn't you agree? When will you do it? Let me know the result as soon as you have it." (This is a serious problem and the sales manager wants to create a sense of urgency.)

Boyd Oil—"Well done. Will you go there with the sample on June 12th?"

"Do you have any concerns about them running the test on that date or soon after—you don't think they'll drag it out?"

Thursday, May 30

Watson Co.—"You said that there wasn't enough volume. How much volume do they do?" ($5,000 per year—American Chemical is looking for new accounts that will generate $30,000 per year as you will recall)

"Even though this is only a potentially $5,000 annual account, wouldn't it make sense to pursue it?" (Probably—it can help build volume)

"Do they plan volume growth over the years?" (The salesperson doesn't know.)

"Wouldn't it make sense to find that out before deciding to abandon this account? (Of course it would.)

Smith Oil—"This looks good. Did McDonald turn out to be the decision maker?" (Yes, he is.)

"Did you find out who the other decision people are?" (Yes, he did.)

"Are you meeting with research to set up the trial test or have research run the test?" (It's set for a meeting.)

"Did you ask McDonald to talk to research and set up the test?" (It's not clear from the call report and it would have been the best strategy, saving one step.) (This Next Action column requires specifics—a date and what will happen. It should have said "run the trial test on 6/20," for example.)

Friday, May 31

Mission Oil—"We talked about this account last Monday. You can see what happens when you don't ask the pre-qualifying questions, can't you? It wastes a call. This was a predictable result."

"What will you do to make sure this kind of thing doesn't happen again?" (The sales manager wants to reinforce the importance of pre-qualifying every situation.)

James Oil—(The salesperson had car problems and there was nothing he could do.)

The call report review is complete. It's time to review the Itinerary for the week of June 3rd. (Figure 6.5)

Monday, June 3

Figure 6.5
Weekly Itinerary/Call Report—Example 3

American Chemical Company – Weekly Itinerary/Call Report

Salesperson *Bob Johnson*

Date	Company Name	Key Contact/Title	Call Objective	Step	Call Result	Next Action
Mon 6-3	ABC Oil	Jack Smith Prod. Mgr	determine if they will consider us	I		
Mon 6-3	Johnson Inc.	Bill Lyons Dir. of Research	Ask him to do a research test	T		
Tues 6-4	Derby Oil	Harry Evans Purchas. Mgr	Ensure proposal reviewed by all	PF		
Wed 6-6	Atkins Oil	Bob Mill Purchasing Mgr	Present proposal ensure dealerse it	PP		
Wed 6-5	Travel to Chicago PM					
Thurs 6-6	Monroe Inc.	Joe Harrington Prod. Supv.	Close the order with DC	C		
Fri 6-7	Agva Oil	Henry Watson Purchasing	Are they satisfied with our supplies	AM		
Fri 6-7	Pure Oil	Joe Bass Purchasing	"	AM		

"Why aren't you making any pre-approach calls today?" (Once, again, there may be a legitimate reason but the sales manager wants to be sure the salesperson keeps the pipeline full—has a sufficient number of new business opportunities to replace the ones that close or are lost orders.)

ABC Oil Co.—"Did they say they would consider us on the pre-approach call? If not, why not?" (It should have been determined on the pre-approach call.)

"If you didn't call Jack Smith, how do you know he'll be there today, and if he'll see you without an appointment?"

"Is Jack Smith the right person to make this decision? Are there others who need to be involved? Who are they?"

Comment: Once again, there may be perfectly good answers to these questions or there may not be. (Recall the situation with Smith Oil on May 30.) The sales manager is making sure that the right things were done. If the answers are not the right ones, the sales manager makes suggestions as to what should be done, up to and including not making the call at all if no pre-approach information was gathered. It is difficult to see important prospects without an appointment in American Chemical's markets.

Johnson Inc.—"Did Bill Lyons commit to a research test on the initial face-to-face call? If not, why not?" (This means it will take two sales calls to accomplish what could have been done in only one—the initial face-to-face call.)

"Were all other qualifying requirements determined on the initial call? Do we know?" (The sales manager will review the qualifying questions with the salesperson to be sure they were asked and to get the answers on this call if they were not—and the sales manager must reinforce the need to ask the commitment question for the next step after every sales call.)

Comment: Again, there may be perfectly good answers to these questions or there may not be. The sales manager is making sure that the right things were done. If the answers are not the right ones, the sales manager makes suggestions as to what should be done as well as what should have been done. Get the commitment for a research test on the initial face-to-face call.

Tuesday, June 4

Derby Oil—"Were copies of the proposal given to all decision people in the first place?"

"Will it be necessary to either talk to each decision person (or get them together) to determine their reaction to the proposal? Couldn't that have been arranged before this call?"

"Aren't we more interested in their reaction to the proposal than simply asking one person if the others have reviewed it?" (Is this really the right objective for this call?)

"You've only planned one call for today? Weren't there any other customers or prospects you could have planned to see while you're in (city)?"

"Is there any one you could cold call?" (If there is, the salesperson might not get to see a decision person but can uncover valuable information about the account—names of decision makers, who they are buying from, and perhaps make an appointment to see one of the decision people either today or in the future.)

Wednesday, June 5

Atkins Oil—"Do you have enough proposal copies for all decision people? When do you expect them all to have reviewed the proposal?"

"Aren't there any other customers or prospects you could have planned to see and traveled to Chicago later in the day?" (One call per day is insufficient at American Chemical; they should plan at least two.)

Thursday, June 6

Monroe Oil—"Is their paperwork ready?"

"Will we have to negotiate anything? If so, what?" (They will discuss on Thursday what American Chemical is willing to give up to get the order today.)

"Do you anticipate any major objections?" (They will discuss possible objections and responses.)

"You've only planned one call for Thursday? Weren't there any other customers or prospects you could have planned to see while you're in (city)?"

"Is there any one you could cold call?"

Friday, June 7

Aqua Oil—"You just called on them last Wednesday? What's the purpose of going back in again so soon?" (The sales manager saw that from last week's call report. There may be a legitimate reason—the sales manager just wants to know what it is—or is the salesperson just making an easy call at the end of the week?)

Pure Oil—"Do you have any concerns about this account?" (The sales manager is simply trying to find out just why the account requires an account management call now—it may or may not be worthwhile.)

Call Report and Itinerary Summary

American Chemical's call report and itinerary will serve as a guide for you to develop one of your own if you believe it to be important. As has been stated, call reports and itineraries are an invaluable sales management tool if used correctly.

The important issue is to review them with your salespeople on a scheduled basis and use them as tools to improve performance. They help identify performance problems and help you strategize with your salespeople, something most salespeople enjoy and need.

It should be obvious that the kinds of information American Chemical's sales managers get allows them to work with their salespeople effectively and efficiently on every account. Without these reports, the process would be helter-skelter at best and selling opportunities would be lost.

Measuring Critical Selling Ratios. Another use for the call report is to measure critical selling ratios. Chapter 5 stressed their importance. You will recall that American Chemical measured the numbers of each of the following that would lead to an order:

1. PA—Pre-approach calls (It's essential to ensure the pipeline stays full.)
2. I—Face-to-face sales contacts
3. Number of qualified prospects (taken from the Call Result column)
4. T—Number of research tests and sales presentations
5. TR—Number of production test runs
6. C—Number of orders closed

This information is easily taken from the call report. American Chemical sales managers "stroke count" the designations in the Step column and qualified prospects from the Call result column. Using the Itinerary and call report (Figure 6.3), the numbers are put onto the Monthly Activity Ratios Report for each salesperson (Figure 6.6).

Each row of boxes is for one week of the month. American Chemical's fiscal quarters run four weeks—four weeks—five weeks so that orders and shipments are always calculated on a Friday. Since every quarter has 13 weeks, it is the simplest method. That is why there are five rows—for the last month of each quarter. Only four rows are completed for May, obviously, since June is the final month of the quarter.

Evaluating these ratios on a monthly basis reveals some things but is not enough time in which to develop a performance pattern. It takes several months of data before a real pattern emerges.

Figure 6.6
Monthly Activity Ratios

Monthly Activity Ratios

Salesperson _Bob Johnson_

Month Ending _May 31st_

Pre-Approaches	Inital Face-to-Face	Number Qualified	Research Tests	Production Runs	Closed Orders
H̶H̶ H̶H̶ II	(II)	II	II	I	—
H̶H̶ H̶H̶ L̶H̶	IIII	II	II	II	—
H̶H̶ H̶H̶ III	II	I	I	—	—
I H̶H̶ L̶H̶	III	I	—	—	—

Month Totals					
Pre-Approaches	Inital Face-to-Face	Number Qualified	Research Tests	Production Runs	Closed Orders
55	12	6	5	3	0

They are transferred to a Yearly Activity Ratios report (Figure 6.7) at the end of each month and forwarded to the national sales manager who tabulates and studies these results for the entire sales force.

Their sales managers now have monthly and year-to-date ratios for each salesperson and can now see how performance stacks up against the standard.

You will notice several things about Bob Johnson from this Report:

Figure 6.7
Yearly Activity Ratios

Yearly Activity Ratios

Salesperson _Bob Johnson_

	Pre-Approaches	Initial Face-to-Face	Number Qualified	Research Tests	Production Runs	Closed Orders
January	42	8	5	2	1	0
February	38	6	4	2	1	1
March	52	10	4	1	0	1
April	49	6	4	3	1	1
May	55	12	6	5	3	0
June						
July						
August						
September						
October						
November						
December						
Annual Totals	236	42	25	13	6	3
Company Average	100% (64)	25% (16)	50% (8)	50% (4)	50% (2)	50% (1)
Salesperson Average	74%	18%	60%	52%	46%	50%

1. His initial face-to-face meeting percentage is lower than standard—18 percent against 25 percent. He may not be calling at the right decision levels or he may be too rigid in his pre-qualifying (ruling out prospects who shouldn't be ruled out).
2. His qualified prospect percentage is better than 50 percent of his initial calls. He obviously has pre-qualified well.
3. His research test percentage is better than 50 percent of his qualified prospects so he qualifies well.
4. His production test runs are almost 50 percent of his research tests. He has qualified all decision people to have gotten this far.
5. His closes are 50 percent of his production test runs.

Bob Johnson is doing a pretty good job. His manager would point out two things from these numbers: a) If he had made 64 pre-approach calls each month and the percentages held (which is a safe assumption), he would have had one more order. b) If he had made Initial face-to-face calls on 25 percent of the pre-approach calls he made, he would have come close to one more order. If he had made Initial face-to-face calls on 25 percent of 320 pre-approach calls (64 per month), he would have had two more orders.

His sales manager is clearly pleased with Bob Johnson's performance but is coaching him on how he can improve his performance by addressing these last two areas.

Activity Ratios Summary. Without this summary of critical selling ratios, the sales manager would not have known what areas to address. As you may recall, Chapter 5 details what problems might exist if these numbers had been very different. Review them.

It should be clear that measuring critical activity ratios is essential to managing sales performance successfully. They determine performance deficiencies and/or improvements. They identify where further training or other types of corrective actions (positive reinforcement memos for above standard or improved performance—a great motivating tool, written warnings for repeated poor performance and terminations). You can and should use them to improve the performance of your salespeople.

Sales Forecasts

American Chemical's salespeople are required to complete and forward a 90-Day Rolling Sales Forecast at the close of each fiscal month (Figure 6.8).

American Chemical wants to see what is expected to close each month and what accounts are expected to close in the 60-day period after that. It allows their sales managers to anticipate, question and

Figure 6.8
90-Day Rolling Forecast

American Chemical Company—90 Day Rolling Forecast
Salesperson Bob Johnson 5/21

Company Name	30 Days	60 Days	90 Days	Step Completed	Prob %	Next Step	$ Value
Monroe Oil	✓			Proposal accepted by all dec. people	90	close order; agree on terms+conditions	42,000 yearly
Atkins Oil	✓			Successfully carry tested the prod. test run	60	present the proposal	27,500 yearly
Daley Oil		✓		Presented the proposal	90	close the order	46,400 yearly
Barton Oil		✓		made sales present, got approval for prod. test.	60	Initiate prod. test prepare proposal	28,000 yearly
Account Totals				$ Totals – 30 67,500 60 64,400 90 0			

discuss strategies to overcome potential obstacles to securing those orders when forecasted. American Chemical's forecast accuracy is roughly 65 percent. That is not bad, but they are constantly trying to improve it.

There are some interesting anecdotes about sales forecasts that will interest you:

1. Many companies require sales forecasts but most are "good guess, wish lists" at best. These companies require it but rarely hold their salespeople accountable while complaining, at the same time, that their salespeople "can't forecast accurately at all."

2. One salesperson told me that his forecasts were what he expected to close, but if they didn't, he would close something else to make up for them. All that mattered to his superiors was that he made the numbers, not whether his forecasts were accurate. If that is the case, then why require a sales forecast in the first place? It's a waste of everyone's time.

3. Sales managers have told me that they get a forecast from their salespeople, cut it in half and forward that to their superior who, in turn, cuts it in half and forwards it to his superior. It's hardly scientific but it's actually done. It has no substance but their companies require a forecast.

4. Some companies tell their salespeople that forecasts are the basis for manufacturing forecasts and that is why they are so important. Very few, if any, companies actually do that. It's simply a way to create some sense of urgency with salespeople to forecast accurately. Most companies would say that they'd go out of business if they relied on their salespeople's forecasts for business planning purposes.

American Chemical requires a forecast for two reasons only. *First*, they want their salespeople to perform each step of the sales process effectively and efficiently. Forecast accuracy is a reflection of that. If forecast accuracy is low, performance problems exist at one or more of their sales process steps. *Second*, they want their sales managers to challenge what has been done at each step to ensure that every account forecasted has met the following criteria:

Probability of 90 percent—All decision people have approved the order and the paperwork is expected to be completed within 30 days

Probability of 60 percent—The production test has been successfully completed and the proposal presented to all decision people

Probability of 30 percent—All decision people have committed to giving American Chemical business if the research and production run tests are successful

If an account doesn't meet these criteria, it is not to be forecasted—period.

Bob Johnson's forecast for the months of June, July, and August raises several serious questions although his numbers have been good to date. Refer to his forecast (Figure 6.8) as comments are made about the accounts forecasted:

Monroe Oil—A sales call is planned for June 6 to close the order—that is to gain agreement to go ahead with the order. On that basis, this account should be given a 60 percent probability. The paperwork is not in process.

It's unlikely that the order will be placed (with paperwork completed) in 30 days. It will more than likely be 60 days since it often takes 30 to 45 days to complete the paperwork.

Atkins Oil—A sales call is planned for June 5 for the purpose of presenting the proposal. Clearly this account can be considered a 60 percent probability since the production test run went well, but it will not become a sales order for at least 60 to 90 days. The proposal must be reviewed, which will take one to three weeks.

When several decision people must give their approval, it is unlikely that they will all do what American Chemical wants them to do in a specific time frame. One or more may be out of town, sick, on vacation or simply preoccupied with other more pressing issues.

Derby Oil—A sales call is planned for June 4 to ensure all parties have reviewed the proposal. You will recall that the sales manager questioned the objective when reviewing that week's itinerary with Bob Johnson. It shouldn't be to see if they have reviewed the proposal but rather have they agreed with and approved it? This certainly should be given a 60 percent probability of closing rather than 90 percent. The product test was successful and the proposal presented. However, it is not closed and the paperwork is not in progress.

The "Next Step" column says "close the order". Johnson can try but he hasn't gotten the decision people's reaction to the proposal. That should be the "Next Step."

Barton Oil—This should be given a 30 percent probability. The production test run isn't completed nor is the proposal. It makes no sense to do the proposal until the production test is completed and all results known.

It most likely won't close in 60 days. Johnson will be fortunate to get the order in 90 days, although that is possible. Barton won't begin the test until June 17, if then. It is unlikely that test results will be complete before the middle of July. The rest of the process will take 45 to 60 days.

The sales manager, with Bob Johnson's agreement, will revise the forecast to reflect what is really most likely to happen.

Forecasting Criteria

One of the keys to successful forecasting is establishing the probability criteria that an order will close. American Chemical's criteria have been reviewed. You should determine what your criteria will be in the spaces below.

You can have as few or as many as you feel is necessary. Remember, the percentage reflects the probability that the order will close, not that "that percentage of the projected dollar volume" will close.

_____ % (Describe your criteria for this percentage.)

_____ % (Describe your criteria for this percentage.)

_____ % (Describe your criteria for this percentage.)

_____ % (Describe your criteria for this percentage.)

Summary—Sales Forecasts

Sales forecasts are important tools to assist you in ensuring that your salespeople effectively and efficiently perform each step of the sales process. Forecast accuracy is a reflection of that. If forecast accuracy is low, performance problems exist at one or more of their sales process steps. You challenge what has been done at each step to ensure that every account forecasted has met your forecast criteria. The sales forecast is an effective development tool if used properly.

Lost Order Report

This is the final report to be discussed. It is essential that American Chemical sales managers know why an order was lost, who the competition was, who won the order, how important price was in the final decision and what the salesperson thinks could have been done differently.

It would be nice to assume that all funnel steps have been performed efficiently and effectively, according to the book. However, things clearly don't always work that way. You can see from Figure 6.9 that price was a much greater factor in the decision than American Chemical thought it would be and that all the decision

Figure 6.9   **Lost Order Report**

Lost Order Report

Date _____ Salesperson _____

Account Name _____

Reason for Losing the Order _____

_____

_____

_____

_____

_____

_____

List all competitors _____

_____

_____

Who won the order? _____

How important was price in the decision? _____

_____

_____

What could have been done differently to win the order?

_____

_____

_____

_____

people were not in their corner. One major player was for the competition right along. Bob Johnson wasn't aware of either.

Other lost order reports might say that American Chemical really didn't perform during the production test run, or the product didn't perform to standard, or they decided to stick with their present supplier to give a few examples. The point is that this report can help keep salespeople focused on future orders more diligently and/or give the company some things to iron out in customer service and product quality, to name just two. It is a wealth of information.

Chapter Summary

This chapter has presented several formal ways to measure the performance of your salespeople. It has discussed:

1. Whether you need to use reports at all
2. How to ensure you only ask your salespeople for reports that are meaningful and why that is so important
3. The kinds of reports you should use and how frequently you should get and use them
4. Examples of those reports (which you can redesign to meet your specific needs)
5. How to use them as performance measurement tools

Sales reports that are reviewed with your salespeople on a scheduled basis are effective tools to:

1. Keep your salespeople focused
2. Identify performance weaknesses (and strengths as well)
3. Know where corrective action is required
4. Strategize about specific account situations to improve your chances of winning the order
    Use them to your advantage.

Chapter 7
Coaching for Improved Sales

C hapters 5 and 6 dealt with identifying performance problems. The objective of Chapter 7 is to introduce methodologies that you can use to help your salespeople improve their performance in those areas where it is below standard—where they are not performing one or more steps of the sales funnel effectively and efficiently. You are the coach.

One of the problems many sales managers encounter when attempting to correct sub-standard performance is getting the salesperson to agree there is a problem. If you have identified a problem with one of your salespeople and he/she doesn't agree that a problem exists, it's all but impossible to correct it. Arguments result and it becomes a "no win" situation for you. Salespeople will say things like:

> "I didn't know I was to develop six new accounts this year."
> "I didn't know I was supposed to attempt to get a commitment from prospects at the end of every call."
> "I think I make enough sales calls."
> "I qualify my accounts well."
> "I follow up on my accounts."
> "I need to spend that much money on entertainment. My customers expect it."

They clearly indicate that these salespeople didn't know what they were supposed to do, or don't think they knew, or didn't let on that they knew.

A well-known management (but not specifically sales management related) book, the *One Minute Manager*, states that when subordinates were asked how well they were doing, the typical response was, "I must be doing all right, I guess, because no one has chewed me out or yelled at me lately. I haven't been told I'm doing a bad job."

The book further states that employees are frustrated when they don't know where they stand with their manager or supervisor, how well or poorly they are doing on the job and what they must do to improve performance. Salespeople are no exception.

The process of mutually setting sales activity goals (discussed in Chapter 5) and measuring them (discussed in Chapters 5 and 6) helps to eliminate those kinds of statements. If your salespeople know what is expected in each of these areas, the sample statements cannot be valid. The kinds of responses given above only occur when there are no agreed upon performance standards. Helping your salespeople improve performance requires that you:

1. Establish a schedule and methodology for regular performance reviews
2. Coach and counsel when appropriate
3. Provide initial and ongoing training (both formal and informal)

This chapter details how to do each of them.

Performance Reviews

Regularly scheduled performance reviews are an important part of the performance improvement process as the name suggests. Chapter 6 emphasized that reports are of little or no value if they aren't followed up both on the phone and in one-on-one meetings with your salespeople.

It was suggested in Chapter 6 that you should set up a phone schedule for each of your salespeople every Monday morning to review their itineraries and call reports and raise any other issues you feel need to be discussed at that time. However, that phone conversation will not be a formal performance review session in the great majority of cases. Some performance issues may come up but typically you will discuss accounts that should close, account strategies, call pattern issues, forecasts, travel planning issues and the like.

This means that there must be specific performance review sessions on a regular basis. Since American Chemical's sales managers know whether their salespeople are meeting sales activity goals or not on a monthly basis, they hold informal monthly review sessions. These are one-on-one meetings with each of their salespeople individually. It is important that it not be done in a group meeting. American Chemical's sales managers used to discuss performance in group meetings but accomplished nothing except to create animosity. No one likes to have his/her performance discussed in front of others. It may seem incredible to you that they did this (it really is insensitive and unproductive) but they weren't the only ones doing it.

The purpose of these sessions is to discuss performance and other issues relating to performance. Before getting into how an actual performance review session should be handled, one other major advantage of these monthly performance reviews must be mentioned. They become the basis for formal annual reviews.

Many companies have a policy of annual (and in some cases semi annual) formal performance reviews. Many (if not most) managers find this process unsettling. I have heard comments like, "Oh boy, it's time to evaluate (salesperson) again." Why is it that so many managers don't like to do it?

It is because the review will be subjective because no performance standards were agreed to and formalized. It is as simple as that. They don't have any idea what to write in the formal review and they anticipate confrontation resulting from salesperson statements like those presented earlier. Almost no one likes confrontation. It's no wonder that so many sales managers don't look forward to annual or semiannual performance reviews.

However, if you have established and gained agreement on performance standards for each of your salespeople and held monthly performance review sessions that by definition become objectively rather than subjectively oriented reviews, the annual review becomes easy. There will be no surprises because your salespeople will evaluate themselves. They know whether they have been performing to standard or not because performance standards were established, agreed to, and reviewed monthly.

These monthly review sessions allow you to gain agreement on actions to be taken to improve substandard performance. As an example, one of American Chemical's salespeople lost an order because of improper follow-up.

Improper follow-up was a recurring problem with this salesperson and the sales manager had discussed it in two previous monthly review sessions but the performance didn't change. This is a common complaint among sales managers—that whatever performance problems are identified, the performance doesn't change even after discussing it with salespeople and saying that there must be a change. Identifying the performance problem is one issue we have addressed. Ensuring it is improved is quite another matter.

There are several questions a sales manager should ask him/herself before attempting to address substandard performance with a salesperson:

1. Is it worth the time and effort? If the answer is yes, then do it. If the answer is no, then a formal warning or dismissal is in order.
2. Does the salesperson know what to do, how to do it, and when to do it? If the answer is no, then training is required. If the answer is yes, then it's time to improve performance.
3. Can the salesperson do it? If the answer is no, the salesperson may be in the wrong job. If the answer is yes, the sales manager is now ready to conduct the monthly review session.

The essence of the review session is to get the salesperson to agree there is a problem when one exists. If the salesperson doesn't think there is a problem, the situation will not be resolved.

In the American Chemical account follow-up issue, the sales manager has not gotten agreement that there was a problem in the previous review sessions. He simply stated that there was a problem and that he expected it to be corrected. In the last review session, he used the proper techniques:

1. Gained agreement that there was a problem
2. Asked the salesperson what suggestions the salesperson could offer to resolve the problem and listened to the salesperson's alternatives
3. Gained agreement on one of the alternatives
4. After the meeting, followed up himself to ensure the performance had improved to standard
5. Praised the salesperson when proper follow-up was performed to reinforce the performance

Following these steps is essential if you want to improve the performance of one or more of your salespeople (or any employee for that matter).

Acme Northeast faced a much different problem. Figure 7.1 shows that Sam's call level was way below the standard. In a performance review meeting prior to the beginning of October, Sam:

1. agreed that his call level was low and that he would improve them to meet the goal.
2. stated that he had personal problems that distracted him for several weeks but that they were behind him.
3. said that he wanted to keep his job with Acme Northeast.

This was the third time Sam had been verbally warned about this problem. He would fix it for a few days and then revert to his old behavior. He was told by management at the end of September that

Figure 7.1.
Accumulative Summary

Sales District 1—Accumulative Summary—Week Ending October 16

Week 3	Bob	Sam	Phyllis	Brian	Phil	Mary	Tom	Totals
980 Calls	869	678	985	936	1,124	963	819	6,374
Difference	-111	-302	+5	-44	+144	-17	-161	-484
Minimum Orders	140	140	140	140	56	28	42	686
Actual	98	59	74	96	50	42	47	466
Difference	-42	-81	-66	-44	-6	+14	+5	-220
Sales Goal	40,194	40,194	40,194	40,194	15,264	8,484	11,158	196,042
Actual	33,810	18,636	28,287	30,483	15,340	9,039	13,656	149,251
Difference	-6,384	-21,558	-11,907	-9,711	-284	+555	+2,498	-46,791
Gross Margin Goal	13,258	13,258	13,258	13,258	5,152	2,800	3,682	64,666
Actual	10,157	6,148	9,096	10,714	4,827	3,027	4,930	48,899
Difference	-3,101	-7,110	-4,162	-2,544	-325	+227	+1,248	-15,767
Calls per Order	9	11	13	10	22	23	17	14
Dollars per Order	345	316	382	318	307	215	291	320
Sales + If Call Goal Met	5,306	9,142	116	7,182	0	401	2,810	24,958

he would be subject to termination if his sales calls were not to standard by the end of October. That is partly why he agreed to improve—he said he didn't want to lose his job.

Obviously, his sales call performance didn't improve and his sales reflect that through the third week in October. Management decided to move another salesperson into Sam's territory and to terminate Sam. It was clear that he couldn't reach his goal by the end of October—in fact, he wasn't even trying.

When he was terminated, he said he understood why but wished he had been given a warning. In fact, he had been given a verbal warning not three weeks prior to his termination. It should have been in writing and Acme Northeast has instituted a policy to issue a written warning if termination is a possibility. If it had been in writing, there would have been no issue.

After he left, one of the other salespeople said that Sam told this salesperson that he knew the goal was 70 outgoing business calls per day but he simply wasn't going to do it. He told management one thing and intended to do quite another.

Acme's weekly Accumulative Summary (Figure 7.1) showed that Sam wasn't even trying to do what he had agreed to do. Termination was the only possible result.

Coaching and Counseling

There will be more discussion on performance reviews further along in this chapter. But since we have detailed the steps to improve performance, it is appropriate to discuss two of the most important tools for improving performance—coaching and counseling in both informal or formal review sessions.

They serve very different purposes. Counseling is designed to get to the bottom of things when a behavior or attitude problem has manifested itself in poor performance. Coaching is designed to rectify an identifiable problem.

Each will be examined in detail

Counseling

Typically, you can't change a salesperson's behavior or attitude, at least not easily. Your job is not to be a psychiatrist—it is to have your salespeople meet performance standards. Attitude or a change in personal behavior will manifest itself in some substandard performance. American Chemical had a salesperson who was going through a divorce and another with alcohol problems.

The former's call levels went way down and sales suffered. The latter didn't show up for work on many occasions and appointments were cancelled or missed without the courtesy of a cancellation. The sales manager wanted to help both of them so he counseled the salesperson going through the divorce to talk with another salesperson who had experienced the same kinds of problems while going through a divorce and to seek outside counseling. Agreement was gained that the salesperson would do both. He counseled the salesperson with the alcohol problem to enter a rehabilitation program at the company expense and take a leave of absence for one month. Both of these salespeople had been good performers in the past and the sales manager wanted them to turn things around so they could become productive people once again.

The key to successful counseling is the ability to uncover the underlying causes of your salesperson's behavior. "Listening" is your most important function in counseling sessions. It is best to prepare a few open-ended questions that allow your salesperson to do most of the talking. It's the only way to find out what's going on.

An important outcome of counseling sessions is to gain mutual understanding. Your salesperson must know what your expectations are—to get outside counseling, take a leave of absence, go on reduced work hours—all depending on the problem. It is obviously in your best interest to save a good performer. However, if the salesperson is to remain on the job (part-time or full-time in the short term), job performance expectations must be set as well. They may be different from the original performance standards but must be established and agreed to if they are different.

One last point about counseling—trying to affect poor behavior by direct means is difficult at best. Although direct intervention may be necessary at times, the results are short-lived. For instance, American Chemical's sales manager noticed the salesperson shaking perceptibly and the prospect shifting uncomfortably in his chair. After leaving the meeting, you point this out and request that he take it easy on the drinking—that it is seriously affecting performance.

Most of the time, your salesperson will modify that behavior, but it will be temporary. Unless you get to the root of this behavior in counseling sessions, there is no way to effect permanent change.

Coaching

Counseling is used to correct specific deficiencies in your salesperson's performance. For example, the American Chemical salesperson's call activity fell way below standard. The sales manager gained agreement with this salesperson that call activity standards would be met while counseling continued. To accomplish this, he used the coaching steps listed earlier and repeated below after determining that the situation was worth the time and effort and that the salesperson knew what to do, when to do it, and how to do it:

1. Gained agreement that there was a problem
2. Asked the salesperson what suggestions the salesperson could offer to resolve the problem and listened to the salesperson's alternatives
3. Gained agreement on one of the alternatives
4. After the meeting, followed up himself to ensure the performance had improved to standard
5. Praised the salesperson when proper follow-up was performed to reinforce the performance

Intrepid Insurance (see Figure 7.2) knew that it took, on the average:

- 20 telephone contacts to get five appointments
- five appointments to get two surveys
- two surveys to get one new policy sold

The owner of Intrepid Insurance identified a problem when she noticed one salesperson would make 20 prospective buyer phone contacts and only get one appointment. This went on for several weeks. She sat with this salesperson for three initial phone contacts and discovered that the salesperson wasn't using the script. Consequently, very few appointments were made.

When she asked the salesperson why the script wasn't used, the reply was that it sounded "canned" and too mechanical. She pointed out the unfavorable appointments to telephone contacts ratio, and the salesperson agreed there was a problem.

The salesperson then stated that the script would be used. It apparently was, because the appointments to telephone contacts ratio immediately improved.

This situation reinforces several of the concepts stressed in this book: *First,* most salespeople need to be kept focused constantly. A few do it on their own but they are the exception. Left to their own devices, most salespeople will stop doing what they know they are supposed to do and do it differently.

The president of Acme Northeast described a salesperson (who had been there only two months) who had also stopped using the introductory script because the salespeople sitting close by had said this salesperson was not natural on the phone. The president said it was amazing how someone new to his industry and markets would defend not using the script that this salesperson knew worked. After

Figure 7.2
The Intrepid Insurance Agency Sales Funnel

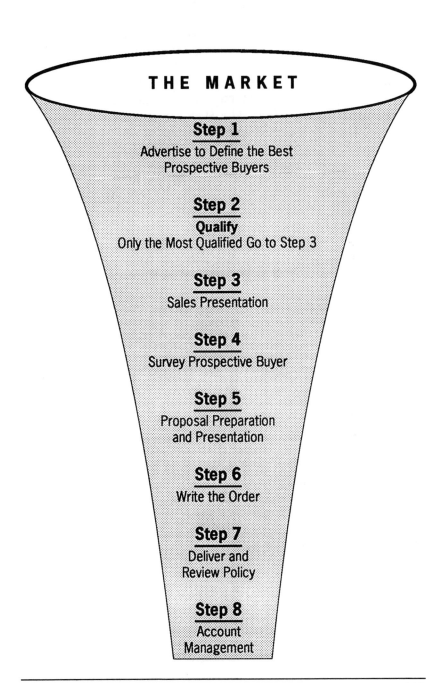

THE MARKET

Step 1
Advertise to Define the Best
Prospective Buyers

Step 2
Qualify
Only the Most Qualified Go to Step 3

Step 3
Sales Presentation

Step 4
Survey Prospective Buyer

Step 5
Proposal Preparation
and Presentation

Step 6
Write the Order

Step 7
Deliver and
Review Policy

Step 8
Account
Management

going back to the script, performance improved. This salesperson was told the following, "You sound unnatural not using the script. If you are going to sound unnatural, you will do it using the script, not your way."

This point was not negotiable. The salesperson had participated in role play sessions where the script was practiced over and over and knew that it was expected to be used. As it turned out, this salesperson became a top-notch performer. But the performance still had to be monitored to ensure focus.

Second, monitoring performance is essential. It can either be done on joint sales interactions or by monitoring performance reports.

Third and finally, take action as quickly as possible when a performance problem exists. Don't waste any time.

Select two of your salespeople who are performing below standard. Describe whether there is a behavior/attitude problem and what the resulting performance problem is specifically, or is it simply a performance problem?

Salesperson #1—Name: _____

Problem: _____

How does it manifest in below standard performance? What is not being done in the sales funnel specifically? _____

_____

Is it worth your time and effort?

Does the salesperson know what is to be done and when?

Does the salesperson know how to do it?

Describe what you plan to do about it using the five coaching steps. _____

_____

Salesperson #2—Name: _____

Problem: _____

How does it manifest in below standard performance? What is not being done in the sales funnel specifically? _____

_____

Is it worth your time and effort?

Does the salesperson know what is to be done and when?

Does the salesperson know how to do it?

Describe what you plan to do about it using the five coaching steps. _____

_____

If you follow the steps you can achieve the results you want. Before continuing with performance reviews, it is important to point out that as a sales manager, it is very difficult to fix a behavior problem. It is much easier to fix a performance problem. It is difficult if not impossible to manage people. You must manage their *performance.*

The Formal Performance Plan

A performance plan should be developed for each calendar year. At the beginning of the plan cycle, performance plan objectives are discussed, mutually agreed upon and documented. These are the activities you expect to be performed in the sales funnel. Both you and your salespeople retain copies. Any changes to the plan during the year should be documented and attached to the performance plan as they occur. In the case of the American Chemical salesperson going through a divorce, the sales manager agreed to reduce sales call activity goals. This was documented and attached to the salesperson's original plan. It must be documented so that no misunderstandings occur in future review sessions.

As has been discussed, monthly "informal review sessions" should be held. The elements of the plan should be discussed. Praise your people for above standard performance and set specific new objectives for correcting substandard performance. These should be documented as well.

At the end of the plan cycle, the performance review should be written and reviewed during an evaluation meeting between you and your salesperson. A salary increase, if there is to be one, should take place at the time of the review session although it is certainly not mandatory. Many companies consider the annual performance review to be the time for salary increases. It does not have to be, especially if performance has been below standard. For example, American Chemical had a salesperson exceed quota for the plan period but whose qualifying and follow-up activities were below standard. There was no salary increase and the salesperson understood why although he was not happy about it.

This raises a very important point. If performance standards are established and agreed to, reviewed during formal or informal monthly review sessions (or as needed if problems surface in between those sessions) and summarized in writing during the formal annual review, there will be no surprises.

Your salespeople know how they have performed so the process becomes objectively rather than subjectively oriented which makes the evaluation not only much easier but more productive as well. You can establish a plan to ensure your salespeople get back to performing to standard when they are not. Performance reviews are a development tool and must be treated as such.

The performance plan cycle begins for the next calendar year by going to Step 1 again.

Performance Plan Format

The performance plan form should include:

1. Performance plan worksheet—a list of the job-specific objectives and job-related accountability
2. Performance review section—measuring performance against the objectives/accountability
3. General performance factors review
4. Development plan (for performance improvement)
5. Employee comments (It is important for the employee to document his/her comments about the review.)
6. Overall rating—against the objectives, not against one another or subjective issues

Figure 7.3 provides an example.

Taking Corrective Action

What action(s) do you take when one of your salespeople is consistently "under the standard?" How long will you "live" with a substandard performer?

It is important to agree on some standardization. For example, if someone is under standard for two months, should he/she be given 30 days, 60 days, 90 days to correct the problem? What happens if it isn't done within the established time frame? In many cases, nothing happens and that creates greater problems: The salesperson doesn't believe you are serious about correcting the problem. Other salespeople on your team see substandard performance continue even after you have tried to correct the problem, which creates morale problems. They will wonder why you haven't addressed the problem, which can begin to undermine your position and authority. Your peers or superiors will begin to wonder about your managerial capabilities.

American Chemical has established several standards for dealing with continuing below standard performance that has resulted in below quota performance:

1. The performance problem(s) is discussed with the salesperson in a review session. A plan to correct the problem(s) is agreed to and the sales manager will followup.
2. If the performance problem(s) continues, the salesperson is given a verbal warning that he/she has 30 days to correct the problem or a termination warning will be written and put in the personnel file. This is put into writing and given to the salesperson.

Figure 7.3   **Performance Plan**
Performance Plan

Objectives
1.   Meet sales quota monthly
2.   Sales call activity 20 per week
3.   Qualify prospective buyers against agreed upon standards (sales funnel Step 2)
4.   Obtain four qualified potential new customers monthly
5.   Add one new customer monthly
6.   Increase existing customer business by 10 percent

Performance Against Objectives—Date:
1.   Achieved 80 percent of quota—below standard—due to sales call activity at 12 per week and only two qualified new potential customers so that the objective of adding one new customer for January was not met.
2.   Increased existing customer business by 15 percent
3.   Sales orders were completed to standard

General Performance Factors Review
1.   You must make more new customer sales call. Not only were your sales calls below the objective but you only made six new customer calls for the entire month.
2.   You are asking the right qualifying questions so meeting the objective is simply a matter of increasing new customer sales calls.
3.   It's obviously much easier to call on existing customers than potential new customers. That is why you increased your existing business above the objective. You did a great job. Keep it up.
4.   Your sales orders for January were done according to company policy. Thats a big improvement over last year. Once again, you did what you agreed to do. Congratulations. I know you'll continue to fill them out correctly.

Development Plan
1.   Increase sales call activity to 20 per week per the objective
2.   Change your call mix so that 50 percent of sales call activity is on potential new customers—10 per week—I will travel with you on five new customer calls per week for the next month to ensure you are comfortable using the initial approach script. Once you are comfortable with it, new customer calls should be much easier to make.
3.   Meet the qualified new customer objective—four in February and close one. I will make closing calls with you.

Salesperson Comments

_____

_____

_____

3. If the problem(s) still continues, the salesperson is given the written warning that he/she will be terminated if the problem is not corrected in 30 days. Roughly 60 days have passed.
4. If the problem(s) still continues, the salesperson is terminated.

This process gives the salesperson 90 days to correct the problem(s). That is an ample amount of time. Some companies take action even faster but American Chemical believes the recruiting, hiring and training investment in their salespeople requires a sufficient amount of time to try to resolve performance problems.

Most typically, however, a substandard performer stays on for months and months and months. Many reasons are given for not taking action earlier. Some of them follow with comments as to why they may be fallacious:

"We have a very long sales cycle, often one year or more, so it takes time for a salesperson to get going."

Comment: That may be true but this sales manager should begin to see levels of funnel activity that predict whether the salesperson will meet or exceed quota very early in the salesperson's career. If they are not at standard, appropriate development or other actions should be taken in review sessions to correct the problem(s).

"I hate to fire someone. It is a tough thing to do and I don't want to hurt the salesperson. Maybe it will work out."

Comment: No one likes to fire an employee. I have never met anyone who does. However, you can be sure that a salesperson who performs below standard for several months after agreeing to improve is not happy in the job. Believe it or not, you are doing the salesperson a favor by terminating him/her. It might not be viewed that way at first but it is better for everyone concerned in the long run.

When you hire a new salesperson, you really know after one to two months whether you have the right person. You will have seen activity in the funnel performed to standard or a sincere attempt to perform to standard. If that is the case, it becomes a development issue. You have someone you can work with.

At this point, an interesting question is raised by most sales managers. What about the consistently above-quota performer who doesn't meet activity standards (like call activity, follow-up activity or product demonstration standards). "What should I do about that situation?" The answer is nothing in most cases. If you determine that this performance could affect quota achievement down the road, some action is required. But it may be that this person can be successful (exceeds quota) without meeting other standards.

Other below-quota salespeople may ask, "Why do I have to meet these standards when he/she doesn't?" My answer is that when they are above quota, they have the right to ask that question. Until then, they will meet the agreed-to activity standards. It is as simple as that.

Training and Developing Salespeople

One of your responsibilities is to train your salespeople. Training focuses on teaching skills and procedures to enable each sales person to perform his/her job to standard. Training is divided into five areas:

1. Induction training—familiarizes newly hired salespeople with the tasks they are expected to perform, and provides them with information about your company regulations and benefits.
2. Product training and product application knowledge
3. Skills training—selling skills, market knowledge, competitive knowledge
4. Remedial training—for those salespeople who exhibit substandard performance in one or more areas
5. Continuous product/applications update training

Training Methodology

Training can be done in a variety of ways: through regularly scheduled sales meetings, one-on-one sessions and joint sales calls. I will discuss each briefly.

Regularly scheduled sales meetings. Determine what training needs are necessary. Develop an agenda and distribute it prior to the meeting (there is nothing worse than a meeting that has no relevance; so ensure it addresses issues of importance to your team).

Get everyone together. The length of the meeting should be determined by travel-time issues and the material to be covered. Typically, no more than four topics should be covered in a one-day meeting so that the impact of the topics won't be diluted.

Have your salespeople suggest meeting topics. Ask one of them with expertise in certain areas to prepare a presentation on that area of expertise. It creates a teamwork atmosphere and learning is enhanced.

One-on-one sessions. These typically would be coaching sessions.

Joint sales calls. This must be done on a regular basis. It's important to make calls at each step of the selling cycle to determine where weaknesses are. As was stated, the "numbers" may indicate that a salesperson either has difficulty qualifying an account or is unable to reach the decision maker(s). You'll need to make a joint sales call to determine which of them is the problem. Or are they both part of the problem?

There are problems with joint sales calls that should be thought of in advance.

The issue of superior selling skills (the tendencies to take over selling situations, unwillingness to let salespeople make mistakes, self-perception as a "super salesperson" rather than as a manager) is a potentially serious one and can create problems on joint sales calls. Individualism (unwillingness to delegate, neglect in developing sales people) is another potentially serious problem. You must answer the following three questions honestly:

First, do you make joint sales calls with your people: to develop their skills, to save an order, or for other reasons?

There will be times when you will make a joint call to save an order. However, the overriding reason should be to observe performance so performance improvement will result in coaching sessions.

Second, how much of your time should be spent traveling with your salespeople? This is an interesting area. Many sales managers say that they don't have enough time to travel with their salespeople, or the salespeople are too far away. However, it is essential that you travel with them. You can determine potential performance deficiencies from the ratio reports, but how will you observe the performance so it can be corrected properly if you don't make joint sales calls? You should make calls with above-standard performers as well as below-standard performers. They need your support and concern as well.

Third, when you make joint sales calls with your salespeople for the purpose of developing their skills, do you ever find yourself "jumping in" and "taking over"?

Consider your answer to the second question from this perspective—if there was the danger that your salesperson would give inaccurate information, or miss an opportunity to zero in on a key selling point, what is the harm? Do you really believe that the damage is done forever, or is there always the chance to go back in and correct the situation afterward?

In most cases, the situation will not kill the sale. And your salesperson will learn from the mistake. We learn more from our mistakes than from our successes. I'm not saying that you should never take over. But it's certainly possible to take over too often.

One of the reasons sales managers take over (and it's for the wrong reason) is that their sales ego is on the line—they know they can do it better, and they miss the selling environment. Don't let your sales ego influence your management style.

Are you willing to let them make mistakes in front of prospects/customers?

Chapter Summary

One of your major objectives is to ensure that your salespeople meet sales goals. Two of the most important tools for improving performance are coaching and counseling. They serve very different purposes: counseling is designed to get to the bottom of things when a behavior or attitude problem has manifested itself in poor performance. Coaching is designed to rectify an identifiable problem.

Note: Neither will be effective if your sales person doesn't agree there is a problem.

Performance reviews (both formal and informal) should be given on a scheduled basis. It is only fair to your salespeople and can help improve performance. They should be objectively rather than subjectively oriented since your salespeople will know when they are performing below standard.

Training for improved performance can be done individually or in group sessions. Training methodologies are detailed in this chapter. Training cannot be a one shot program. I have had sales managers tell me that a salesperson went through a basic selling seminar one year ago and is trained. That is like saying that a person who has been taught to drive a standard shift automobile for two days, with both instructions and practice, is skilled at it. It takes longer than that. It takes continual practice until driving a standard shift car becomes second nature. It is the same for salespeople. The proper selling skills/strategies and ability to perform sales funnel activities effectively and efficiently will not take root in a one to two or even three-day training session. It takes time and practice.

Train your salespeople, expect them to make mistakes, monitor their performance and then train them to do it properly—as many times as is necessary to get it right. They now know why the training is so important so they are much more receptive, assuming they can do it and want to do it.

Chapter 8
More Sales Funnels

Throughout this book you have seen a wide range of sales organizations using sales funnels. The concept is clearly applicable to every type of selling environment and the matter of qualifying early in the process is fundamental. The only sales funnel shown where face-to-face qualifying was not done is the direct mail house where qualifying, to the degree that it could be done, was in the selection of the mailing list.

This chapter shows four new sales funnels. They were not a part of the companies presented and discussed in Chapters 2 through 5.

Figure 8.1 shows a personnel recruiting organization, specializing in the placement of human resource professionals. Their recruiters must sell companies and applicants on the value of using their services and properly match qualified applicants to specific human resource job openings. It requires a great deal of skill.

To keep the sales funnel full, their recruiters must be working with a specified number of well-qualified client companies and potential candidates developed from a wide variety of client companies and potential candidates.

R. D. Gatti Sales Funnel

The R.D. Gatti sales funnel (shown in Figure 8.1) is similar to all other businesses in the qualifying step. They must determine who will give them the best "openings" opportunities and which applicants are best qualified (even if it means searching out applicants who aren't looking for a new opportunity). They must manage the client/applicant relationship until the position is filled. Their reputation depends on success—successfully qualifying in both directions.

Banking Services Sales Funnel

In this case, the bank is selling payroll, lock box and 401K plans and services. (See Figure 8.2) Their customer base is used to develop potential small to medium-business clients for these services. The

Figure 8.1
R. D. Gatti & Associates Inc. Personnel Recruiters Sales Funnel

bank sells its services by effectively qualifying potential clients. It is their most important step since they have so many prospects. They initially qualify by phone and then set an appointment for a face-to-face sales call.

As you formulate steps for the goals of your salespeople, keep in mind one other aspect: that all the successful companies you have

Figure 8.2
Banking Services Sales Funnel

read about used sales funnels over a period of time. Be faithful to your plan and insist that your salespeople devote *time* to each step.

Real Estate Sales Funnel

The real estate firm's sales funnel has similar qualifying questions to all other businesses. (See Figure 8.3) They must find qualified sellers and qualified buyers in a very competitive marketplace.

Figure 8.3
Real Estate Firm Sales Funnel

Assisting with financial arrangements and negotiating with both parties are very important steps in their process.

Commercial Printing Company Sales Funnel

The Commercial Printing Company's qualifying step is similar to all other businesses. (See Figure 8.4) Some small jobs can be sold on the phone (especially with existing customers) but some larger and

more complex jobs require face-to-face sales calls to present services
and review customer requirements.

Figure 8.4
Commercial Printing Company Sales Funnel

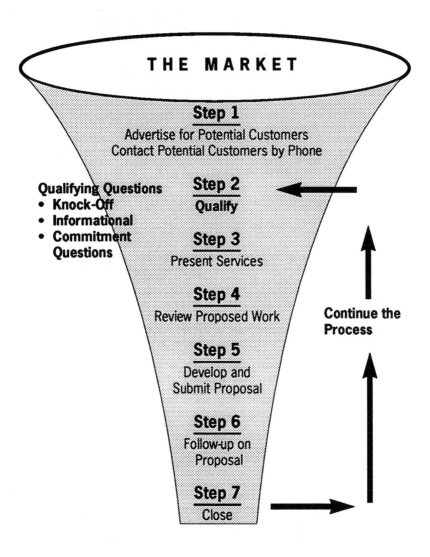

Summary

Successfully managing sales performance means you must develop and manage an effective and efficient sales management system. That system is a product of identifying the steps that comprise your sales funnel or process, establishing performance standards and activity levels and, finally, ensuring your salespeople have the skills to move through the steps in that process effectively and efficiently.

This book has attempted to provide the framework within which you could develop your sales management system, your model of the successful sale. It has given you the tools to establish performance standards and activity levels, and the tools to measure performance and take appropriate actions to correct substandard performance.

You cannot manage results. If you don't address critical sales system issues until your salespeople miss assigned sales volume targets, you are much too late. The horse is out of the barn. Shutting the door now won't help.

You cannot manage people. Managers can only manage performance. Sales managers can only manage the sales performance of their salespeople at each step of the sales process (including submitting reports, attending meetings and other job-related performances).

Salespeople want to know exactly what they are expected to do and how they will be measured. A selling "system" is the only means by which to fairly and accurately evaluate performance. And, a well-managed system will yield positive results. The lack of a system yields inconsistent and random results.

If you manage the system you have developed from this book, sales productivity will improve. You must be aware, however, that some salespeople will balk at the system. It is new to them and, for some, old habits are hard to break. For others, being measured at each step of the process is frightening. They don't want to be held accountable for performance standards at each sales process step. So it may take time to get the system up and running to your satisfaction.

Don't give up on it is the point being made. Stay with it until it does work to your satisfaction. Sales results are your responsibility, and you are accountable when they are below standard. You must hold your salespeople accountable as well.

Your sales management system is the methodology. Use it successfully.

Index